Economic Psychology
of Travel and Tourism

Economic Psychology of Travel and Tourism

John C. Crotts
W. Fred van Raaij
Editors

The Haworth Press, Inc.
New York • London • Norwood (Australia)

Economic Psychology of Travel and Tourism has also been published as *Journal of Travel & Tourism Marketing*, Volume 3, Number 3 1994.

The development, preparation, and publication of this work has been undertaken with great care. However, the publisher, employees, editors, and agents of The Haworth Press and all imprints of The Haworth Press, Inc., including The Haworth Medical Press and Pharmaceutical Products Press, are not responsible for any errors contained herein or for consequences that may ensue from use of materials or information contained in this work. Opinions expressed by the authors(s) are not necessarily those of The Haworth Press, Inc.

The Haworth Press, Inc., 10 Alice Street, Binghamton, NY 13904-1580 USA

Library of Congress Cataloging-in-Publication Data

Crotts, John C.
    Economic psychology of travel and tourism / John C. Crotts, W. Fred van Raaij, editors.
        p.   cm.
    Includes bibliographical references and index.
    ISBN 1-56024-705-3
    1. Tourist trade–Psychological aspects. 2. Travelers–Psychology. I. Raaij, W. Fred van. II.
Title.
G155.A1C76 1995
338.4'791'019–dc20   94-23527
                                                                               CIP

INDEXING & ABSTRACTING

Contributions to this publication are selectively indexed or abstracted in print, electronic, online, or CD-ROM version(s) of the reference tools and information services listed below. This list is current as of the copyright date of this publication. See the end of this section for additional notes.

- *ABSCAN, Inc.*, P. O. Box 2384, Monroe, LA 71207-2384

- *Centre des Hautes Etudes Touristiques (CHET)*, IMMEUBLE EUROFFICE, 38 av. de l'Europe, 13090 Aix-en-Provence, France

- *Journal of Health Care Marketing (abstracts section)*, Georgia Tech-School of Management, Ivan Allen College-225 North Avenue NW, Atlanta, GA 30332

- *Leisure, Recreation & Tourism Abstracts (LRTA/CAB ABSTRACTS)*, Cab International, Wallingford, Oxon OX10 8DE, England

- *Lodging & Restaurant Index*, Purdue University, Stone Hall Room 220, West Lafayette, IN 47907-1002

- *Management & Marketing Abstracts*, Pira International, Randalls Road, Leatherhead, Surrey KT22 7RU, England

- *Sage Urban Studies Abstracts (SUSA)*, Sage Publications, Inc., 2455 Teller Road, Newbury Park, CA 91320

- *Social Planning/Policy & Development Abstracts (SOPODA)*, Sociological Abstracts, Inc., P. O. Box 22206, San Diego, CA 92192-0206

- *Sociological Abstracts (SA)*, Sociological Abstracts, Inc., P. O. Box 22206, San Diego, CA 92192-0206

- *Sport Database/Discus*, Sport Information Resource Center, 1600 James Naismith Drive, Suite 107, Gloucester, Ontario K1B 5N4, Canada

- *The Hospitality Index*, Quanta Press, Inc., 1313 Fifth Street SE, Minneapolis, MN 55414

- *Urban Affairs Abstracts*, National League of Cities, 1301 Pennsylvania Avenue NW, Washington, DC 20004

(continued)

SPECIAL BIBLIOGRAPHIC NOTES

related to special journal issues (separates)
and indexing/abstracting

☐ indexing/abstracting services in this list will also cover material in the "separate" that is co-published simultaneously with Haworth's special thematic journal issue or DocuSerial. Indexing/abstracting usually covers material at the article/chapter level.

☐ monographic co-editions are intended for either non-subscribers or libraries which intend to purchase a second copy for their circulating collections.

☐ monographic co-editions are reported to all jobbers/wholesalers/approval plans. The source journal is listed as the "series" to assist the prevention of duplicate purchasing in the same manner utilized for books-in-series.

☐ to facilitate user/access services all indexing/abstracting services are encouraged to utilize the co-indexing entry note indicated at the bottom of the first page of each article/chapter/contribution.

☐ this is intended to assist a library user of any reference tool (whether print, electronic, online, or CD-ROM) to locate the monographic version if the library has purchased this version but not a subscription to the source journal.

☐ individual articles/chapters in any Haworth publication are also available through the Haworth Document Delivery Services (HDDS).

Economic Psychology of Travel and Tourism

CONTENTS

ABOUT THE EDITORS

John C. Crotts, PhD, is Assistant Professor in the Department of Recreation, Parks, and Tourism at the University of Florida. He also serves as Director of the Center for Tourism Research and Development which coordinates and facilitates the research activities of faculty concerned with travel and tourism development and management. Dr. Crotts regularly consults with and has performed funded research projects on tourism matters for numerous private, local, state, and federal organizations.

W. Fred van Raaij, PhD, is Professor of Marketing in the Department of Management at Erasmus University in Rotterdam, The Netherlands. His research interests include consumer behavior, especially consumer decision processes and the role of affect; advertising psychology; consumer confidence and expectations, spending, and saving; poverty and unemployment; and tourism and recreation. Dr. van Raaij edited the *Journal of Economic Psychology* for 10 years and has been an editorial board member for several professional publications.

Preface

This volume was designed to present papers on economic psychology that include implications for travel and tourism, their economic processes, implications and management. This issue has sought to stimulate new approaches in the study of travel and tourism by providing a forum for the exchange of information and ideas between European and North American researchers. Papers are included which report on either empirical studies or contribute to the conceptual and theoretical perspectives of the sociopsychological mechanisms that underlie travel and tourism demand and the economies of destinations.

This volume is aimed at two different audiences: (1) students of tourism; and (2) travel and marketing professionals. Students in tourism programs often receive a good background in psychology and in marketing. However, there are seldom efforts to link the two disciplines. Fundamental areas in psychology such as the formation of attitudes, beliefs and motivations, and the social influences on the individual are seldom framed in terms of tourists' consumptive behavior. Tourism marketing courses, on the other hand, have a tendency to focus narrowly on the marketing mix as it influences consumers at or near the point of sale. Seldom do they address the broader economic-psychological issues that impact both the supply and demand sides of the travel and tourism economy over the long haul. For instance, how consumers perceive and react to information about vacation destinations. This volume hopefully fills in these omissions by addressing relevant issues in the strategic marketing of tourism.

Travel researchers who are engaged in advancing the tourism economy will find here the opportunity to review applications of psychological theories and methods to the study of travel and tourism phenomena. Hopefully, this will generate further dialogue among social scientists in Europe

---

[Haworth indexing entry note]: "Preface." Crotts, John C., and W. Fred van Raaij. Published *in Economic Psychology of Travel and Tourism* (ed: John C. Crotts, and W. Fred van Raaij), The Haworth Press, Inc., 1994, pp. ix-x. Multiple copies of this article/chapter may be purchased from The Haworth Document Delivery Center [1-800-3-HAWORTH; 9:00 a.m. - 5:00 p.m. (EST)].

and North America in recognizing the areas of psychology, economic and social psychology in particular, that can help us deal with the fundamental issues underlying the travel and tourism economy.

John C. Crotts
W. Fred van Raaij

Introduction:
The Economic Psychology
of Travel and Tourism

W. Fred van Raaij
John C. Crotts

INTRODUCTION

Psychology is of crucial importance for the development of economic theory, the practice of marketing, and research on travel and tourism. One should take into account the results of research on human behavior, because people react upon the economic conditions as they perceive them rather than objectively defined conditions. The perception, evaluation and consequent decision-making of consumers may be biased. Humans are neither perfect decision-makers nor utility-maximizers. Economic psychology provides evidence about the behavior of consumers that is instrumental for the development of economic theory as well as for marketing, consumer policy, and research on tourism and travel. More generally, economic psychology offers an interdisciplinary framework in which the methods and theories from the disciplines of economics and psychology can be used to explain the economic behavior of individuals and groups.

Economic psychology is the interdisciplinary development from the side of psychology, mainly cognitive and social psychology (Van Raaij,

W. Fred van Raaij is affiliated with the Rotterdam School of Management, Erasmus University, Rotterdam, The Netherlands. John C. Crotts is associated with the Department of Recreation, Parks and Tourism at the University of Florida, USA.

[Haworth indexing entry note]: "Introduction: The Economic Psychology of Travel and Tourism." van Raaij, W. Fred, and John C. Crotts. Published in *Economic Psychology of Travel and Tourism* (ed: John C. Crotts and W. Fred van Raaij), The Haworth Press, Inc., 1994, pp. 1-19. Multiple copies of this article/chapter may be purchased from The Haworth Document Delivery Center [1-800-3-HAWORTH; 9:00 a.m. - 5:00 p.m. (EST)].

1

1991). Handbooks on economic psychology are Antonides (1991), Furnham and Lewis (1986), Lea, Tarpy and Webley (1987), MacFadyen and MacFadyen (1986), and Van Raaij, Van Veldhoven, and Wärneryd (1988). The development from the side of economics is called behavioral or psychological economics. See the books by Earl (1988), Gilad and Kaish (1986a, 1986b), Katona (1975), and Scitovsky (1976, 1986).

Wärneryd (1988) defines economic psychology as "A discipline that studies the social-psychological mechanisms that underlie the consumption of products and services and other economic behavior. It deals with consumer preferences, choices, decisions and factors influencing these behaviors, as well as the consequences of decisions and choices in the satisfaction of needs. Furthermore, it deals with the impact of external economic phenomena upon consumer behavior and well-being. Studies may relate to different levels of aggregation, from the individual and household to the macro level of entire nations" (p. 9). Economic psychology is not only concerned with the foundations of economics and the development of economics or behavioral economics as a science. It has also provided useful information on human economic behavior in general, and, what we will see in this volume, tourist behavior in particular.

The purpose of this volume is to give an overview of economic psychology as applied to the study of travel and tourism. This volume can be seen as an attempt to claim certain scientific problem areas in travel and tourism as constitutive of psychology in general and economic psychology in particular. This paper is organized as follows. First we review the theoretical developments in economic behavior, schools in psychology, and economic psychology as to their relevance to the study of tourism. Next, we highlight the articles in this volume that employed selected applications of economic-psychological theory in travel and tourism research contexts. Juxtaposed in this overview are areas of economic psychology that are applicable to the study of tourism, but have only received minimal attention in the literature. Lastly, we discuss the role of information in consumer decision making. Moreover, we present a theoretical framework for understanding the function and processing of information in vacation decision making in an attempt to guide and influence research aimed at understanding the decision rules that facilitate the decision task.

ECONOMIC BEHAVIOR

What economics and economic psychology have in common is that they both try to describe, to explain, and possibly to predict economic behavior at the individual and the aggregate level. Economics is mainly concerned with the prediction of economic behavior at the aggregate level, and with direct relations between inputs and effects (e.g., between income, prices, and purchases) (Covington, Thunberg and Jaureqia, 1994) or between advertising expenditure and increase in sales. However, psychological variables such as perception and evaluation, intervene between inputs and effects.

Economic behavior is human decision and choice behavior with regard to the alternative use of scarce resources (e.g., money, time, effort, space, material resources, and energy) to satisfy needs. For instance, the discretionary income available for travel, the weeks or days one can allocate for a vacation, and availability of choice alternatives are examples of resources allocated by consumers. Consumers allocate these scarce resources in an attempt to generate a satisfactory level of utility. The scarcity of means is expressed in the constraints posed by financial, time, effort and other budgets.

Some substitution between these budgets is possible. One could, for instance, increase the financial budget at the expense of time and effort budgets by working overtime. The choice among alternative uses of resources may be regarded as a matter of cost/benefit trade-offs, in which the concept of costs and benefits should be enlarged to encompass a 'behavioral' dimension as well (Verhallen and Pieters, 1984). The behavioral costs are the effort, delay and psychic costs of behavior and behavioral change. Planning and organizing one's own vacation involves behavioral costs, although it is acknowledged that many people derive emotional benefits from the trip planning process. Norms and values play a role in the allocation of resources (Etzioni 1988a, 1988b), choices between competing alternatives (Pitts and Woodside, 1986) and in the confrontation of cultures if vacationers are visiting foreign countries.

An integrated economic-psychological behavioral theory should be developed. According to this theory, the actor (person, consumer, manager, or tourist) performs a more or less elaborated decision process, in which not all relevant information can be acquired and/or processed. Information about alternatives is often not available and generally considered symbolic in nature since the qualities and characteristics of a tourism service cannot be assessed until actual use (Crotts and Guy, 1993). Advertisements only provide positive information about the products or services provided. Complete information, or sometimes even a necessary level of information, is unattainable or unavailable in a market, because of the opposing objectives of the market parties. Sometimes it is even dysfunctional to collect complete information (e.g., in emergency situations and in settings where the supply of 'best' alternatives is limited).

The psychological model of economic behavior supports the notion that actors under conditions of high involvement try to behave rationally, but seldom succeed, because of constraints of availability of information and processing constraints. Simon (1963) introduced the concept of bounded rationality. People try to be rational within the boundaries of their possibilities.

If the search for information is incomplete or not all information is available at the same time, a simplification of the decision process called 'satisficing' is the best which can be done. It is another concept introduced by Simon (1963). It is simply impossible to find the single 'best' alternative, as utility maximization theory suggests. The 'best' vacation destination does not exist. Tourists know that they may select another destination next year to compensate for a less optimal choice this year. Satisficing is seeking to attain a certain aspiration level. If the performance falls below this level, search behavior is induced and the aspiration level is adjusted downward, until goals reach attainable levels.

The economic motivation of people is often not to maximize short-term utility. In many cases it is motivated by continuation of the household and the avoiding of enduring problems. As Lindblom (1959) asserts, it is a muddling-through process. The decision to buy a second home may take years until one suddenly is confronted with an attractive alternative (Stewart and Stynes, 1994).

Economic behavior, and tourist behavior in particular, is almost always motivated behavior. It is guided by preferences, expectations, goals, values and norms. It has a certain level of activation or involvement, and a certain direction. Persons try to reach a goal or to avoid negative consequences. Economic psychology, as a study of economic behavior, tries to explain behavior by learning and decision processes, motivation, personality factors, perception, preferences, and a number of other factors basic to behavior. These processes may be explicit and extensive in the case of high-involvement decisions involving where to vacation. In other cases, these processes are routine and implicit, such as in the case of low-involvement decisions about buying a soft drink.

Learning processes may either precede or follow an economic decision. Take for example the purchase of a recreational vehicle or a vacation on a cruise ship. Learning processes before the purchase pertain to the selection and choice among alternatives. Learning processes after the decision relate to justification and dissonance reduction. Not only the choice alternatives as such, but also situational factors, such as the constraints to freedom and perceived presence of other persons, play a role in the decision process.

SCHOOLS IN PSYCHOLOGY

Psychology is less of a unitary science than economics. One should be aware that there are a number of 'schools' of psychology which represent different approaches to the explanation of behavior. The four major approaches are behaviorism, psycho-analysis, cognitive and social psychology. As a metaphor, one could relate these approaches to three levels in the brain. Behaviorism is concerned with the brain stem, studying reflexes, learning as conditioning and habits. Psychoanalysis is concerned with the limbic system, studying drives, emotions, and the unconscious. Cognitive psychology is concerned with the neocortex, the new brain, studying more complex learning processes and information processing. The three approaches are discussed as to their relevance for economic psychology, travel, and tourism.

The behavioristic approach starts from observable behavior as determined by external and internal stimuli. Learning takes place, if responses are connected with stimuli, either by association, repetition or reinforcement. In behaviorism, mental constructs such as 'attitudes,' are excluded or avoided as much as possible. Alhadeff (1982) developed a psychological foundation of economic theory, based on Skinner's theory of instrumental learning (reinforcement). The behavioristic approach is useful in the study of spontaneous associations induced by advertising (classical conditioning), reinforcements consumers receive from the use of products and services (operant conditioning), and social learning by observing and imitating others.

Scitovsky (1976) based his approach on Berlyne's notion of psychological arousal and stimulation level. This is often called the physiological school in behaviorism. The basic tenet is that people strive for an optimal level of stimulation. People engage in travel and tourism either to increase their stimulation level by having new and novel vacation experiences, in case of boredom; or to reduce their stimulation level, in case of stress.

Optimal arousal theory provides an extended framework for understanding the need for psychological stimulation. Based upon several lines of evidence (see Iso-Ahola, 1980 for a literature review) the individual has been shown to possess a need for both security and change. If an environment is perceived as providing too much change or incongruity, the individual will attempt to avoid or withdraw from that setting. On the other hand, if the individual perceives an environment as too familiar, the individual will quickly tire of that setting and will seek more arousal through incongruent, novel or complex situations. Therefore a complex decision task is a dialectical and optimizing process between two opposing forces, the need for stability and the need for change. Crotts (1993) provides evidence that vacation decisions are simultaneously channeled between an individual's conflicting needs for security and arousal.

The psychoanalytical approach (Freud, Adler, Jung) attributes an important role to subconscious motives and desires. Dichter's (1964) approach is an example of a psychoanalytical theory of consumer behavior. Early juvenile experiences and repressed sexual desires tend to influence later behavior, although people may not be aware or are unwilling to admit these effects. The psychoanalytical approach is difficult to test, although it may provide interesting explanations for the interaction of partners during travel, or perhaps the allure of brothels for some patrons.

The third approach is cognitive psychology, in which complex learning and choice processes and the role of memory are the central themes. Bettman (1979) provides an overview of this approach to the study of consumer behavior. Especially in the 1970s, the cognitive approach was popular in consumer research (Hansen, 1972). Decision processes can be modelled to select the best option or (in economic terms) to maximize utility.

A school within cognitive psychology is Lewin's (1935) field theory. Behavior is a function of several forces (valences) in a behavioral field. Lewin (1935) influenced Katona (1975) in his approach to economic psychology. The study of 'consumer sentiment' (optimism and pessimism) is a central topic in Katona's research. Consumer sentiment, as a climate of opinion, is an important factor explaining consumer spending, borrowing and saving at the aggregate level, especially for discretionary products and services. Since a vacation trip represents a discretionary product, it can be delayed or skipped, when consumers are pessimistic about the future.

Social psychology is concerned with the effect of others on one's behavior and with the formation and functioning of groups. Many concepts from social psychology (e.g., attitude, attribution, social comparison, reference group) are used in economic psychology. Travel and tourism is strongly influenced by social factors and referent persons. Take, for example, the importance placed on word-of-mouth communication and complaining behavior.

In recent research approaches, affect (emotion) is taken into account, normally in a cognitive model. Affect influences decision processes and plays a role as a factor in the processes of perception and evaluation (van Raaij 1989; Pieters and van Raaij, 1988). Norms and values often have an affective connotation (Etzioni, 1988a, 1988b).

ECONOMIC PSYCHOLOGY

Whereas micro-economics and behaviorism assume a direct relationship between stimuli and responses, Katona (1975) introduced the intervening factor of the organism (person) with its perceptions and preferences. Stimuli must be perceived and evaluated, before they elicit responses or have an effect on responses. Individuals differ in their perception and evaluation of reality and act according to their perceived/evaluated reality and not to the stimuli as such. Economic perceptions and evaluations are not random deviations from a 'correct' value and will not cancel out at the aggregate level. But they show systematic changes, reinforcing or influencing the business cycle. The prediction of economic responses will thus be improved by adding information on consumer or entrepreneur evaluations and expectations.

Katona (1975) developed the Index of Consumer Sentiment (ICS) for this purpose, as an indicator of consumer optimism and pessimism. Since the late forties in the U.S.A. and since 1972 in Europe regular surveys are held to measure consumer optimism and pessimism. Some survey questions pertain to the general economic situation, such as inflation, employment and the evaluation of the economic situation; other questions relate to the household economic situation, saving and making ends meet. From five of these survey questions, the ICS is computed. The ICS in combination with income data contributes to the explanation and prediction of consumer spending, saving, and borrowing. In periods of consumer optimism, spending and borrowing increases; in periods of consumer pessimism, saving increases. For an analysis of the ICS with Dutch data since 1972 (see van Raaij and Gianotten, 1990). The ICS is a leading indicator of change in consumer sentiment and the direction of change of U.S. travel volume (Crotts, Thunberg, and Shifflet, 1992).

Katona's ICS is, however, not the only variable that can wedge itself between stimulus and response. Perception, evaluation and expectation can each become an intervening variable between stimulus and response. In addition, after the response (i.e., purchasing behavior) an evaluation takes place as to whether the vacation expectations were met. This may lead to (dis)satisfaction, repeat visits or not, or complaints and negative word-of-mouth communication.

Van Raaij (1981) developed a meta-model in which psychological variables intervene between the economic variables. The economic environment as perceived by the economic actors is influenced by personal factors such as dispositions, optimism and pessimism. The perceived economic environment and situational factors affect economic behavior. Subjective well-being has impacts on the economic environment and this closes the cycle of Figure 1. Psychological variables, thus, intervene between the economic environment and economic behavior, and between economic behavior and the economic environment.

A third contribution of economic psychology is to increase the set of explanatory variables by adding psychological variables to the set of economic variables. A vacation depends on both the consumer's ability and the willingness to purchase. In other words, once consumption is not constrained by the ability to pay, the issue becomes social-psychological in nature. In settings where neither branch of the literature would be sufficient to explain certain phenomena, a combination of the two affords the researcher considerably more latitude in addressing economic problems and variations in consumer behavior. For example, to explain variations between households' allocations toward vacationing, one could add

FIGURE 1. A model of economic-psychological relationships (van Raaij 1981).

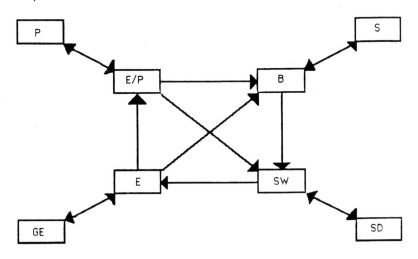

GE = General Economic Conditions
E = Economic Environment
P = Personal Factors
E/P = Perception of Economic Conditions
B = Behavior
S = Situation (events in the environment)
SW = Subjective Well-being
SD = Societal (system) discontent

managerial skills and internal control of the household members to economic variables, such as net income and contractual obligations. The economic variables describe the economic possibilities and constraints of the household (Frey and Foppa, 1986). The psychological variables describe the motivation, willingness and abilities of the household within these constraints. The combination of both provides an excellent insight in the dynamics of household decision making. Adding the ICS (willingness) to income data (possibilities) to explain consumer expenditure is another example of this conjunction.

Economic psychology either adds new variables to increase explained variance, provides a better operationalization of the concepts, suggests intervening variables for a better understanding of the relationships, or provides a new and better frame of interpretation of the problems under study.

SELECTED APPLICATIONS
OF ECONOMIC-PSYCHOLOGICAL RESEARCH

Tourism behavior manifests itself in many forms. As it is impossible to describe all areas of economic-psychological research that are relevant to tourism, this discussion is limited to a number of areas. The effects of consumer sentiment on consumer expenditure including recreation and vacation has been previously discussed. Areas such as human values and travel decision making and the psychology of entrepreneurial innovation, although applicable, are not included in this discussion nor the volume at large. In these applications, psychological variables may contribute to a better understanding of economic behavior than by economic variables only.

Product Perception

Consumer perception of the product or service is an important element of marketing and promotion. The 'touristic product' is often a combination of subproducts and services centered around a destination environment. These product components are produced, packaged and distributed by several organizations. For example, tour operators and travel agencies combine a destination's attractions, transportation, lodging, food and beverage components into a single product to be sold to consumers. With a well-known brand name added, the product gains in value, trust, and reliability for consumers. The central theme of van Rekom (1994) is product perception and differentiation in tourism. How are concrete attributes related to touristic motivations and values?

Consumer Behavior

The most developed part of economic psychology is the study of consumer behavior, especially as applied to marketing. Here the economic-psychological approach has added considerably to the micro-economic theory of consumer behavior. Price and income elasticities are used in conjunction with a host of psychological and sociological factors. Consumer information processing and social influence are dominant approaches. The psychological approach has almost replaced micro-economic theory in marketing. From a marketing perspective, buyer behavior is a central topic. From an environmental and home-economics perspective, usage and disposition behavior are central topics. Dimanche and Havitz (1994) discuss four topics in consumer behavior such as involvement and novelty seeking and its relevance and application to travel and tourism research.

Consumer Decision Making

A topic of particular concern is the study of consumer decision making, both at the individual and group decision making levels. The decision making process may be described in terms of its decision rules or by combining information about choice alternatives in order to find the 'best' alternative (i.e., the alternative with the highest preference or utility). Bettman (1979) provides an overview of this line of research. As vacation trips are important priorities for many individuals and families, the decision making process about the next vacation is usually extensive. Jenkins (1978) studied the roles and influence of family members on vacation decision-making. Gitelson and Kerstetter (1994) study the influence of non-family members in travel decision-making. A qualitative study on consumer choice is by Stewart and Stynes (1994) in their study of the extensive decision process to buy a seasonal home.

Household Production

Household production is a neglected topic in economics. Official statistics do not account for household work, an important area of production, especially during economic recessions. Household production is related to the informal economy. The Beckerian (1981) approach has been amplified with psychological factors. Recreation and vacation are important areas of household production. People spend money, time, and effort on activities in their free time and 'produce' benefits for themselves and their families.

Advertising Effects

Advertising research, mainly as part of marketing, is concerned with the impact of advertising on attitude, cognition and behavior. Economics could only explain relationships between advertising budgets and market shares. An example of this approach is Crouch's (1994) study on promotion and demand in international tourism. The psychological approach provides a better insight into how the process of advertising works. The interaction between affective and cognitive factors in an advertising message has received considerable attention (van Raaij, 1989). Goossens (1994) studies the effects of touristic direct mail involving experiential information.

Business Behavior

The study of entrepreneurial behavior has some similarities with consumer behavior, especially the buying and investment behavior of business-persons (Sheth, 1977). In addition to the economic approach, Simon (1955), for instance, investigated organizational decision making with the concepts of 'satisficing' and aspiration level. Tax compliance is another aspect of business behavior. An example of a study on tax compliance is given by Crotts and McGill (1994).

Tax Behavior

Taxation and its avoidance and evasion is an enduring research interest of economic psychologists (Lewis, 1982). Crotts and McGill (1994) extend from this literature in their exploration of the issues related to noncompliance with local option lodging taxes. Since much of local government support for tourism is derived from lodging tax revenue, the issue is not only relevant for the convention and visitors bureaus that are funded by lodging tax revenues, but also hoteliers who are responsible to collect the tax. Several fundamental issues emerge from the literature that extends beyond descriptive measures of tax compliance rates. For example, do hoteliers perceive a fiscal connection between their collection of lodging taxes and local government spending of these revenues? To what degree do hoteliers consider the tax system as equitable and fair? Which norms and values towards a local option tourism development tax prevail? Which factors influence individual tax complying behavior (Kinsey, 1986)? Based on economic utility theory, economists would recommend increase of penalty in case of noncompliance. Economic psychologists would recommend improving the fairness and fiscal connection between who is required to collect the tax and how tax revenues are used.

Consumer Satisfaction

Consumer satisfaction after the purchase is a relative concept, focussing on the discrepancy between the expectations and actual performance of the product or service (Schouten and van Raaij, 1990). Together with the study of consumer complaints and consumerism, it has more or less become a separate field of research, related to consumer policy. Given the influence of word-of-mouth on vacation decisions, it is surprising so little attention has been given to visitor satisfaction and its relationship to tourism demand (Perdue and Pitegoff, 1990). Andreasen (1977) provides a review of research on consumer satisfaction and its implications for government and business.

CONSUMER INFORMATION PROCESSING AND DECISION MAKING

What is information? Information is often described as relevant data about choice alternatives (e.g., their scores on attributes or characteristics). The data become information, if they prove relevant for someone attempting to make a better choice among competing alternatives. Information may be in a spoken, written or pictorial format, and may come from personal, commercial, or neutral sources.

Information may serve the decision maker in several ways (van Raaij, 1988):

1. Consumers may expect a better decision outcome after information acquisition, processing, and retrieval.
2. Information may reduce the perceived risk of the choice.
3. Consumers may feel more confident after using information, although their decision is not necessarily better.
4. Information is needed to trade off the present costs and expected future benefits of information processing.
5. Information processing may be useful in finding desirable alternatives or ruling out undesirable ones.
6. Information may be used in an ego-defensive way to justify one's behavior after the actual decision has been made.

In economic behavior, as in most other behavior, decision making is a process of evaluating alternatives and selecting one or more (or none) 'optimal' alternative(s). The decision may be at a generic level ('whether to go on vacation or not'), a modal level ('what type of vacation'), or a specific level ('which destination or which travel agency'). A generic decision is largely based on the time, financial budget and general benefits. Alternatives are not easily comparable in a generic choice situation. Often alternatives can only be compared at an abstract or experiential level. Modal and specific decisions generally require more specific information on the attributes of the alternatives under consideration. This information is acquired from internal and external sources.

Internal and external search for information should be distinguished. Internal search of information stored in memory employs information from previous learning and experience that may be suitable for similar decisions. The search for information from external sources involves information obtained from four basic sources: (1) personal (e.g., friends and relatives), (2) mass media (e.g., print and electronic), (3) neutral (e.g., travel clubs, travel guides, travel consultants), and (4) retailer sources (e.g., store visits). Beatty and Smith (1987) found that external search for information is larger with high product involvement but low product class knowledge, with positive attitudes toward shopping, and with ample available time. Apart from active search for internal and external information, people may be confronted with information they did not search for, and learn consciously or unconsciously from it. This is called incidental learning.

Consumers may expect to make a 'better' decision after information acquisition and processing, due to a cultural norm that all decisions should be based on reason and documentation. See Etzioni (1988a, 1988b) for an opposing view, that decisions are based on normative and affective factors. Compliance with this cultural norm of rationality will generally be stronger for 'important' decisions, involving a major financial outlay or affecting other persons. Impulsive behavior is seldom valued, except in settings involving spontaneous gift giving.

Normative approaches to decision making presume that collecting and comparing information and 'structuring the problem' will help the decision maker. Decision aiding does not only help in making the decider aware of all aspects of his/her decision, but may also influence the decision making process. Borcherding (1983) distinguishes between a normative and a prescriptive approach. In a normative approach, generally accepted decision goals are defined for an optimal decision. In a prescriptive approach, subjective decision goals are defined in order to reach an optimal decision for the subject.

Economic decisions inherent in a vacation are often characterized by a financial, temporal and/or effort risk. For some decisions, a physical risk becomes relevant (e.g., crime on tourists in Miami, attending the festival for the bull in Madrid, consuming food and drink in an underdeveloped country). Many decision makers feel more confident after acquiring information, even if this information is not really processed to reach the decision (Oskamp, 1965). For example, consumers gain confidence from nutritional information on the packages, although they may not fully understand this information.

The function of information in increasing confidence with the outcome may be dysfunctional for a better decision (i.e., the 'illusion of knowledge'). Jacoby and his co-researchers (Jacoby, Speller, and Kohn, 1974a, 1974b) and van Raaij (1977) find that consumers use only a small part of the available information but are more confident with their decision, if much information is available to them. The quality of the decision may even decrease under conditions of information overload, since irrelevant information obscures the access to relevant information.

On the one hand, consumers have the 'right' to have access to relevant information, although information overload may have its dysfunctional effects. This is due to the human limitations in encoding, storing, and retrieving this information; to the human limitations in information processing; and to the fact that relevant information is often confounded with irrelevant information. From a consumer policy perspective, one should carefully design ways of information presentation for consumers, in such a way that 'optimal' decisions are facilitated.

Information acquisition and processing involves behavioral, and sometimes even financial costs. Financial costs include travel and telephone costs; behavioral costs include the time and effort spent to obtain the information. These financial and behavioral costs are often traded off against the expected gain of information and the expected future benefits of a better decision. In shopping behavior, not only the price of a product, but also travel time, costs and effort should be considered in comparing shopping trips.

Economic decision makers often process information on the costs and benefits of information processing. In this 'thinking about thinking' decision makers assess whether it is worthwhile to acquire and to process information, and how much information to process. The cost of information may provide important insight to researchers who often find that many travelers report no information search in their vacation planning process.

The 'cost of thinking' (Shugan, 1980) is related to the similarity and complexity of the alternatives. It is relatively 'costly' to decide between similar alternatives or between alternatives with many attributes or characteristics. However, it is not always necessary to process all information that is available. 'Heuristics' and simple decision rules may facilitate the decision task, although one is not certain in this case to obtain the 'optimal' alternative.

CONCLUSIONS

Psychology as a science developed later than economics. Therefore it is not surprising that the economic approach of assumed utility-maximization dominated for a long time in theoretical developments concerning economic behavior. The situation has changed now. The explanatory power of models of economic behavior could be increased by adding and integrating psychological variables, especially those from cognitive and social psychology, into models of economic behavior (Frey, 1983). This is most clear in the study of consumer behavior, in which psychological variables play an increasingly important role. It is also emerging as a promising area of research in the study of travel and tourism.

This volume is aimed at two different audiences: Students of tourism and travel and marketing professionals. Students in tourism programs often receive a good background in psychology and in marketing. However, there are seldom efforts to link the two. Fundamental areas in psychology such as the formation of attitudes, beliefs and motivations, and the social influences on the individual are seldom framed in terms of tourists' consumptive behavior. Tourism marketing courses, on the other hand, have a tendency to focus narrowly on the marketing mix as it influences consumers at or near the point of sale. Seldom do they address the broader economic-psychological issues that impact both the supply and demand sides of the travel and tourism economy over the long haul. This volume hopefully fills in these omissions by addressing relevant issues in the strategic marketing of tourism.

Travel researchers who are engaged in advancing the tourism economy will find here the opportunity to review applications of psychological theories and methods to the study of travel and tourism phenomena. Hopefully, this will generate further a dialogue among social scientists in Europe and North America in recognizing the areas of psychology and social psychology theory that can help us deal with the fundamental issues underlying the travel and tourism economy.

ACKNOWLEDGEMENTS

First, we would like to thank the authors for their contributions. Each paper went through a thorough and lengthy review process that quite often required considerable changes in the papers. We thank the authors for promptly making these necessary changes in time for the editorial deadlines.

Second, we are indebted to the reviewers whose thorough and constructive comments contributed greatly to the quality of the final papers. These reviewers were:

Kathleen Andereck, Arizona State University, U.S.A.
Gerrit Antonides, Erasmus University, Rotterdam, The Netherlands
Larry Guske, North Carolina State University, U.S.A.
Ady Millman, University of Central Florida, U.S.A.
Richard R. Perdue, University of Colorado at Boulder, U.S.A.
Tom Potts, Clemson University, U.S.A.
Laurel Reid, Brock University, U.S.A.
Stephen F. Witt, University of Wales, Swansea, U.K.

REFERENCES

Alhadeff, D.A. (1982). *Microeconomics and Human Behavior*. Berkeley, CA: University of California Press.

Andreasen, A.R. (1977). A taxonomy of consumer satisfaction/dissatisfaction measures. *Journal of Consumer Affairs, 11*, 11-24.

Antonides, G. (1991). *Psychology in Economics and Business*. Dordrecht, The Netherlands: Kluwer Academic Publishers.

Beatty, S.E., and S.M. Smith (1987). External search effort: An investigation across several product categories. *Journal of Consumer Research, 14*, 83-95.

Becker, G.S. (1981). *A Treatise on the Family*. Cambridge, MA: Harvard University Press.

Bettman, J.R. (1979). *An Information-Processing Theory of Consumer Choice*. Reading, MA: Addison-Wesley.

Borcherding, K. (1983). 'Entscheidungstheorie und Entscheidungshilfeverfahren für komplexe Entscheidungssituationen (Decision theory and decision aids for complex decision situations).' In: M. Irle (Ed.), *Methoden und Anwendungen in der Marktpsychologie*. Göttingen, FRG: Verlag für Psychologie, Dr. C.J. Hogrefe, pp. 64-173.

Covington, B., E. Thunberg and C. Jauregui (1994). Modelling growth in international demand for travel to the United States. *Journal of Travel & Tourism Marketing, 3* (3).

Crotts, J.C. (1993). Personality correlates of the novelty seeking drive. *Journal of Hospitality & Leisure Marketing, 1*(3), 7-29.

Crotts, J.C., and B.S. Guy (1993). The relationship between retail advertising and published quality ratings of hotels and motels. *Proceedings of the 1993 Academy of Marketing Science Conference*, Miami Beach, FL.

Crotts, J.C., E.M. Thunberg, and D.K. Shifflet (1992). Consumer confidence as a leading indicator of change in U.S. travel volume. *Journal of Travel & Tourism marketing, 1*, 53-62.

Crotts, J.C., and G.A. McGill (1994). Tax compliance in the U.S. lodging industry: Theory, measurement strategies and findings. *Journal of Travel & Tourism Marketing, 3* (4).

Crouch, G.I. (1994). Promotion and demand in international tourism. *Journal of Travel & Tourism Marketing, 3* (3).

Dichter, E. (1964). *Handbook of Consumer Motivations.* New York, NY: McGraw-Hill.

Dimanche, F., and M.E. Havitz (1994). Consumer behavior and tourism: Critique and extension. *Journal of Travel & Tourism Marketing, 3* (3).

Earl, P. (Ed.) (1988). *Psychological Economics.* Dordrecht, The Netherlands: Kluwer.

Etzioni, A. (1988a). Normative-affective factors: Toward a new decision-making model. *Journal of Economic Psychology, 9*, 125-150.

Etzioni, A. (1988b). *The Moral Dimension: Toward a New Economics.* New York: The Free Press.

Frey, B.S. (1983). *The economic model of behavior: Shortcomings and fruitful developments*, Working paper, University of Zürich, Switzerland.

Frey, B.S., and K. Foppa (1986). Human behaviour: Possibilities explain action. *Journal of Economic Psychology, 7*, 137-160.

Furnham, A., and A. Lewis (1986). *The Economic Mind. The Social Psychology of Economic Behaviour.* Brighton, Sussex: Wheatsheaf.

Gilad, B., and S. Kaish (Eds.) (1986). *Handbook of Behavioral Economics, Volume A, Behavioral Microeconomics.* Greenwich, CT: JAI Press.

Gilad, B., and S. Kaish (Eds.) (1986). *Handbook of Behavioral Economics, Volume B, Behavioral Macroeconomics.* Greenwich, CT: JAI Press.

Gitelson, R., and D. Kerstetter (1994). The influence of non-family members in travel decision-making. *Journal of Travel & Tourism Marketing, 3* (3).

Goossens, C. (1994). Goossens, C. (1994). External information search: Effects of tour brochures with experimental information. *Journal of Travel & Tourism Marketing, 3* (3).

Hansen. F. (1972). *Consumer Choice Behavior. A Cognitive Theory.* New York: Free Press.

Iso-Ahola, S.E. (1980). *The Social Psychology of Leisure and Recreation.* Dubuque, Iowa: Wm.C. Brown.

Jacoby, J., D.E. Speller, and C.A. Kohn (1974a). Brand choice behavior as a function of information load. *Journal of Marketing Research, 11*, 63-69.

Jacoby, J., D.E. Speller, and C.A. Kohn (1974b). Brand choice behavior as a function of information load: Replication and extension. *Journal of Consumer Research, 1*, 33-42.

Jenkins, R.L. (1978). Family vacation decision-making. *Journal of Travel Research, 16* (4), 2-7.

Katona, G. (1975). *Psychological Economics.* New York: Elsevier.

Kinsey, K.A. (1986). Theories and models of tax cheating. *Criminal Justice Abstracts*, *18*, 403-425.

Lea, S.E.G., R.M. Tarpy, and P. Webley (1987). *The Individual in the Economy. A Textbook of Economic Psychology*. Cambridge, U.K.: Cambridge University Press.

Lewin, K. (1935). *A Dynamic Theory of Personality*. New York, NY: McGraw-Hill.

Lewis, A. (1982). *The Psychology of Taxation*. Oxford: Martin Robertson.

Lindblom, C.E. (1959). The science of muddling through. *Public Administration Review*, *19*, 79-88.

MacFadyen, A.J., and H.W. MacFadyen (Eds.) (1986). *Economic Psychology: Intersections in Theory and Application*. Amsterdam: North Holland.

Oskamp, S. (1965). Overconfidence in case-study judgments. *Journal of Consulting Psychology*, *29*, 261-265.

Perdue, R. R. and B. E. Pitegoff (1990). Methods of accountability research for destination marketing. *Journal of Travel Research*, *Vol. 28* (1), 45-49.

Pieters, R.G.M., and W.F. van Raaij (1988). Functions and management of affect: Applications to economic behavior. *Journal of Economic Psychology*, *9*, 251-282.

Pitts, R.E., and A.G. Woodside (1986). Personal values and travel decisions. *Journal of Travel Research*, *25*, 20-25.

Schouten, V., and W.F. van Raaij (1990). Consumer problems and satisfaction in a retail setting. *Journal of Consumer Satisfaction, Dissatisfaction and Complaining Behavior*, *3*, 56-60.

Scitovsky, T. (1976). *The Joyless Economy. An Inquiry into Human Satisfaction and Consumer Dissatisfaction*. New York: Oxford University Press.

Scitovsky, T. (1986). *Human Desire and Economic Satisfaction*. Brighton, Sussex: Wheatsheaf.

Sheth, J.N. (1977). 'Recent developments in organizational buying behavior.' In: A.G. Woodside, J.N. Sheth and P.D. Bennett (Eds.). *Consumer and Industrial Buying Behavior*. New York, NY: North-Holland, pp. 17-34.

Shugan, S.M. (1980). The cost of thinking. *Journal of Consumer Research*, *7*, 99-111.

Simon, H.A. (1955). A behavioral model of rational choice. *Quarterly Journal of Economics*, *69*, 99118.

Simon, H.A. (1963). 'Economics and psychology.' In: S. Koch (Ed.), *Psychology: A Study of a Science*. New York: McGraw-Hill, pp. 685-723.

Stewart, S.I., and D.J. Stynes (1994). Toward a dynamic model of complex tourism choices: The seasonal home location decision. *Journal of Travel & Tourism Marketing*, *3* (3).

van Raaij, W.F. (1977). Consumer information processing for different information structures and formats. *Advances in Consumer Research*, *4*, 176184.

van Raaij, W.F. (1981). Economic psychology. *Journal of Economic Psychology*, *1*, 1-24.

van Raaij, W.F. (1988). 'Information processing and decision making. Cognitive aspects of economic behavior.' In: W.F. van Raaij, G.M. van Veldhoven, and K.E. Wärneryd (Eds.), *Handbook of Economic Psychology.* Dordrecht, The Netherlands: Kluwer Academic Publishers.

van Raaij, W.F. (1989). How consumers react to advertising. *International Journal of Advertising, 8*, 261-273.

van Raaij, W.F. (1991). 'Economics and psychology.' Chapter 40 in: D. Greenaway, M. Bleaney and I.M.T. Stewart (Eds.). *Companion to Contemporary Economic Thought.* London/New York: Routledge, 1991, pp. 797-811.

van Raaij, W.F., and H.J. Gianotten (1990). Consumer confidence, expenditure, saving, and credit. *Journal of Economic Psychology, 11*, 269-290.

van Raaij, W.F., G.M. Van Veldhoven, and K.E. Wärneryd (Eds.) (1988). *Handbook of Economic Psychology.* Dordrecht, The Netherlands: Kluwer Academic Publishers.

van Rekom, J. (1994). Adding Psychological Value to Tourism Products. *Journal of Travel & Tourism Marketing, 3* (3).

Verhallen, T.M.M., and R.G.M. Pieters (1984). Attitude theory and behavioral costs. *Journal of Economic Psychology, 5*, 223-249.

Wärneryd, K.E. (1988). 'The psychology of innovative entrepreneurship.' In: W.F. van Raaij, G.M. van Veldhoven, and K.E. Wärneryd (Eds.). *Handbook of Economic Psychology.* Dordrecht, The Netherlands: Kluwer Academic Publishers.

Adding Psychological Value to Tourism Products

Johan van Rekom

SUMMARY. The motives of tourists are deeply rooted in their pattern of expectations, goals and values. The laddering technique is used in order to investigate this pattern. It provides a basis for positioning strategies. The promised experience has to be realized by means of concrete activities on the shop floor. Existing goals and values serve to motivate employees to adopt activities required for meeting the tourists' expectations. If, after the purchase of a package, the members in the production chain with which the tourist is confronted, differ in mentality, each individual organization appropriate goals must be introduced. Then successful product differentiation will be possible.

THE COUNTER-EVERYDAY TOURISM EXPERIENCE

Tourism provides the consumer with an experience which consists of an escape from everyday life. Jafari and Gardner (1991) describe the phenomenon of tourism as a series of alternating long ordinary periods and short non-ordinary periods in one's lifetime. As the stress of daily routine comes to color someone's feelings, one yearns for refreshment. Jafari and Gardner compare the experience of a tourist with the experience of the

---

Dr. J. van Rekom is Assistant Professor in Tourism at Erasmus University Rotterdam, Faculty of Management, Department of Marketing Management. P.O. Box 1738, 3000 DR Rotterdam.

[Haworth co-indexing entry note]: "Adding Rsychological Value to Tourism Products." Van Rekom, Johan. Co-published simultaneously in the *Journal of Travel & Tourism Marketing* (The Haworth Press, Inc.) Vol. 3, No. 3, 1994, pp. 21-36; and: *Economic Psychology of Travel and Tourism* (ed: John C. Crotts, and W. Fred van Raaij), The Haworth Press, Inc., 1994, pp. 21-36. Multiple copies of this article/chapter may be purchased from The Haworth Document Delivery Center [1-800-3-HA-WORTH; 9:00 a.m. - 5:00 p.m. (EST)].

21

reader of a book. In the same way the reading of a book does, tourism offers a "counter-everyday" non-ordinary experience. The tourist's goal is to encounter some variation of the aesthetic experience, whose features include not only beauty, elevation, illumination and the like, but also such familiar things as adventure, settings and deep or free feelings. The tourists' means to reach this goal are the elements of the trip they are making; hotels, restaurants, monuments, exotic beaches, pleasant waiters and so on. Armed with both motives and means, the tourist leaps off on a journey to the land of the non-ordinary, unknown, or even horrific (Jafari & Gardner, 1991).

The means for this journey are provided by the tourism industry. Their societal function lies in making the non-ordinary experiences accessible to the stressed consumer. They supply the product elements which are essential in the implementation of travel and vacations. But tourism is a highly competitive industry with little apparent differentiation in products. Product differentiation which could give tourists their longed-for extraordinary experience does not appear to have reached its full development. Products of many tour operators, hotels and airlines are to a fairly high degree interchangeable, and the paradoxical situation occurs that dreams are sold on the criterion of price.

The purpose of this paper is to investigate the relation between the way tourists think to realize their dreams and the tourist industry's potential to make those dreams come true.

TOURISTS' GOALS AND VALUES

The tourist product, or better said service, involves many very tangible properties–down to the size of the hotel bed. These properties vary from situation to situation, and are very different for diverse types of vacations, as well as for diverse tourists going on vacation. Their value added is not in the down-to-earth details, but rather in the out-of-daily life experience which they have to sustain. This experience is bought at a travel agency, or more directly at suppliers more upstream in the tourism production chain, like hotels or camping sites. Tourists will try to satisfy their needs by assembling different elements of the tourism product.

A central tourist need which has been revealed time and again in empirical research is the 'escape' notion. In a large German research project, the most frequently quoted vacation motives were 'to relax' (by 71.7 % of the respondents) and 'to escape from daily routines,' quoted by 66.9 % of the respondents (Braun & Lohman, 1989). Robie, Bateson, Ellison and Figler (1993) compared two larger tourist motivation surveys, the Travel Motivation Survey and the Tourist Canada Travel Survey. They found that one of the three common factors motivating travel was 'the need to escape,' followed by 'to experience the new and different culture' and 'jetsetting, prestige seeking.' Whereas 'jetsetting' refers to achieving status by having something done rather than to undergoing a certain experience, 'culture' entails a certain experience value.

Tourists contrast their travel experience with their daily life, out of which they have developed the cultural baggage (Liebman Parrinello, 1993) which delivers them the criteria to evaluate and to enjoy this experience: these goals or values which they strive for, but which they do not manage to attain in their daily life. In tourism literature these are often referred to as 'needs.' Direct translations of empirical research results into specific products are difficult, mainly because of the general nature of the studies published. Questions generally unanswered are, how variable are tourist motives and to what extent are they prompted by different types of tourist experiences (Mannell & Iso-Ahola, 1987). So far, the apparent heterogeneity of travel experiences, motives and needs is too cumbersome to provide a general answer to these questions. It might be more workable to look for the specific answers to each specific situation.

Iso-Ahola (1984) proposed a two-dimensional framework to analyze tourists' motivations. Two main factors simultaneously influence the individual's leisure behavior. The first is the escape factor; engagement in leisure and tourism activities allows one to leave one's daily environment behind. The other motivational factor is the individual tendency to seek psychological rewards from participation in leisure activities. Iso-Ahola further divides both factors into personal and interpersonal. Mannell and Iso-Ahola (1987) emphasize that any leisure activity, including tourist behavior, has those two components. The two components of escaping and reward seeking, however, are not really independent. Escaping, in essence, is seeking gratification of those values which are not being realized in daily life. It is, rather, a component in the much larger encompassing framework of reward seeking.

Pitts and Woodside (1986) found a significant relation between people's personal values and the choice of travel destinations, but no clear relationship between salient choice criteria which people used and the value orientations. The question remains, how tourists themselves translate their goals into concrete choices. Witt and Wright (1991) point out, that knowledge of needs alone will not necessarily tell us what people will actually do to fulfill them, or indeed whether they will do anything at all. It requires an understanding of the processes whereby these needs are transformed into motivated behavior, and, in particular, of the way in which people's expectations give motivated behavior its direction. If we want to know how their choices relate to the more general goals and values, we have to investigate which rewards are sought and by which means. Then the exact association patterns can be identified which play a role in a specific choice situation. The 'laddering technique' (Reynolds & Gutman, 1984) has especially been developed for this purpose.

THE LADDERING TECHNIQUE

In the early 1980s, Reynolds and Gutman (1984) developed the 'laddering' technique. The essence of this technique is that consumers are asked for the concrete choice criteria they think important when choosing a product, for instance a vacation trip. Figure 1 shows the outcome of a hypothetical vacation study. Tourists are asked what elements they think are important criteria in the choice of a vacation. They may mention, for instance, that they want to have their travel documents at home at least one week before departure. This is important to them, because this means that everything is well organized (following the line upward from the box 'documents at home a week before departure'). When they are asked, why it is important that 'everything is well organized,' they answer, that then they will have nothing to worry about. And 'nothing to worry about,' in its turn, is important in order to be 'really on vacation,' which in its turn leads to the still higher value of 'the need to relax.' Following the lines in the figure, which are also called 'means-ends chains,' it is possible to determinate which concrete choice criteria serve to reach which higher values. The higher in the map, the more general and more important the goals and values become. Reynolds and Gutman called this kind of figure a 'Hierarchical Value Map' (HVM).

INVESTIGATING THE POTENTIAL
TO MEET THE TOURIST'S CRITERIA

Such a figure gives useful information about the elements which are important in the tourists' choice of a certain product (in this case a summer vacation) and helps the organization to position itself and to organize its communication. In communication, the company can stress one of the elements in the HVM which the consumer considers highly relevant. Consumers themselves will make the association with their own higher level values, the 'driving forces' (Olson & Reynolds, 1984). An organization

FIGURE 1. Hypothetical Hierarchical Value Map for a summer holiday.

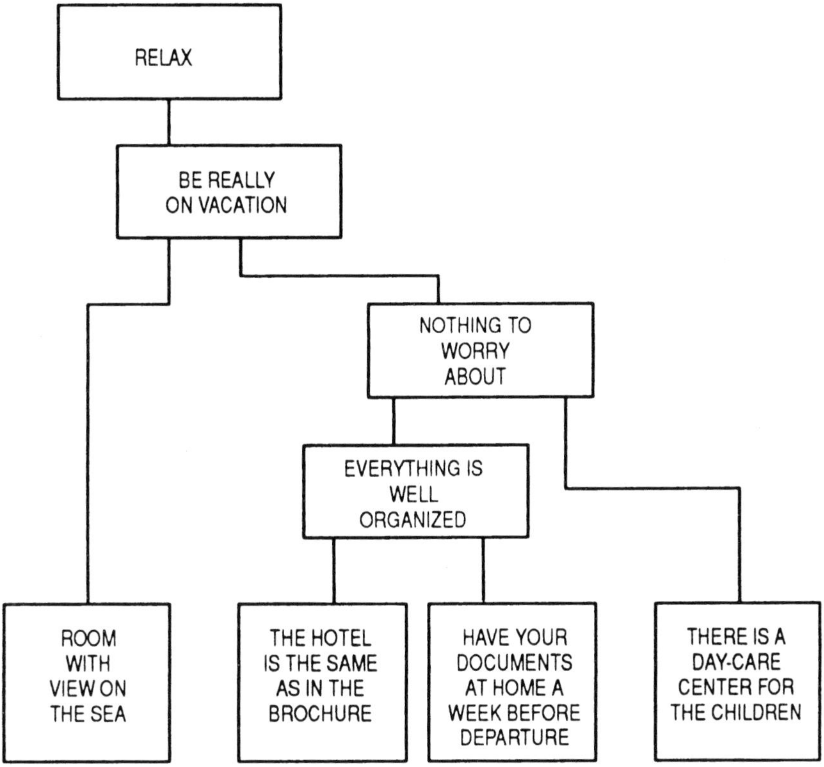

```
┌─────────────────────┐
│                     │
│   RELAX             │
│                     │
└─────────────────────┘
           │
    ┌──────────────┐
    │  BE REALLY   │
    │  ON VACATION │
    └──────────────┘
           │         │
           │    ┌──────────────┐
           │    │  NOTHING TO  │
           │    │   WORRY      │
           │    │   ABOUT      │
           │    └──────────────┘
           │         │           │
           │    ┌──────────────┐  │
           │    │ EVERYTHING IS│  │
           │    │    WELL      │  │
           │    │  ORGANIZED   │  │
           │    └──────────────┘  │
           │      │        │      │
┌──────────┐ ┌──────────┐ ┌──────────┐ ┌──────────┐
│ ROOM     │ │THE HOTEL │ │HAVE YOUR │ │THERE IS A│
│ WITH     │ │IS THE    │ │DOCUMENTS │ │DAY-CARE  │
│ VIEW ON  │ │SAME      │ │AT HOME A │ │CENTER FOR│
│ THE SEA  │ │AS IN THE │ │WEEK      │ │THE       │
│          │ │BROCHURE  │ │BEFORE    │ │CHILDREN  │
│          │ │          │ │DEPARTURE │ │          │
└──────────┘ └──────────┘ └──────────┘ └──────────┘
```

may for instance choose to position itself on the theme 'nothing to worry about.' The tourists draw the conclusion that if they have nothing to worry about, they really will be on vacation. Figure 1 also shows how very concrete elements in an HVM can be relevant to realize the goal, in the tourists' case the experience they long for. For instance, the presence of a day-care center for children is important, because in consequence, tourists will have nothing to worry about, not even as regards their children.

A tourism product can be perfectly positioned in the mind of the consumer by means of the selling agent's communication. But then the promised experience still has to be realized. In the example of Figure 1, the clients should indeed receive a vacation free of worries. The management of the business can enhance or destroy the value of the tourism experience (Calantone & Mazanec, 1991). The organizations involved in organizing and executing the journey all have to be able to live up to the promise, and to turn the fantasy into reality–at least in part. Effort is required of all companies involved, especially on the operational level of the drivers, hostesses and guides to realize the promised experience. One careless bus driver can spoil the whole idea of the tourist having 'nothing to worry about.' If the vacation does not respond to the raised expectations, the tourist may perceive it as an unfair purchase, and this is an important factor in determining dissatisfaction (van Raaij & Francken, 1984).

Living up to the choice criteria is a minimum requirement, which will prevent dissatisfaction. This does not mean that organizations should only try to meet the expectations. Tourists, in general, are diving into the unknown and will not realize all consequences before they start the trip. Leisure motives or needs measured before a given leisure experience are different from the same measurements taken after the leisure experience (Mannell & Iso-Ahola, 1987). Only when they are already traveling do they learn what the new environment they looked for really brings them, and what elements in that environment will have what consequences for them. For instance, tourists traveling in the winter to southern England may not notice until they are on the trip that the weather may be really cold and chilly there, or that in certain picturesque quarters of a Mediterranean town they feel less safe than they felt when seeing the photographs. They may also discover that a 'horchata,' a cold almond drink which so far has been unknown to them, is a delicious refresher in a hot Spanish town, or that the new French superfast train system changes the perceived distances between cities. Tourists learn on the road. As a consequence, after-the-trip experiences never match the before-the-trip motivations completely. There is plenty of room for surprise, pleasant or unpleasant, as they will meet on their way more elements which provide them with unforeseen experiences and their consequences. Nice surprises come about when organizations offer unexpected product elements which help the tourists in realizing their goals and values. If an organization has adopted the realization of such goals as one of its own targets it can stimulate and use the creativity of its own employees to systematically create such surprises.

In enterprises in the service industries, such as hotels and travel agencies, where the communication between the employee and the guest is very intensive, a favorable, less favorable or even unfavorable impression is very quickly formed. The entrepreneurial success of an enterprise philosophy is closely related to the enterprise culture (Kaspar, 1989); the positioning of an organization or their service product can only be successful if both management and employees are willing to implement the positioning actively. That is to say, that the whole corporate identity of each organization involved must be structured to help the tourists realize their dreams, and, better still, provide for activities which pleasantly surprise the tourist's goal and value system.

THE CORPORATE IDENTITY OF TOURISM ORGANIZATIONS

'Corporate identity' has been defined as 'the total of signals an organization emits to its stakeholders' (van Rekom, 1993). It embraces every activity of an organization. Organizational actions originate at the level of the individual. Direct contact with the consumer does not as a rule take place at management level, but at the level of waiters, guides and drivers, as part of the function they perform within the organization. Everybody working in an organization contributes to its identity.

Strictly speaking, the organization's identity boils down to the signals emitted by the individual employees in their jobs within that organization. The more concrete signals are the employees' concrete acts. By means of these acts employees want to realize their goals and values, consciously or not. Behavioral acts may be very variable, depending upon the circumstances. The goals and values at which they are aimed are the more constant elements which regulate the behavior to a certain extent. Achieving the goals and values, therefore, will enable the researcher to grasp the enormous heterogeneity of everything a company does in a relatively concise number of terms. For this purpose, the means-end structure behind the concrete signals can be traced. Goals and values are realized to a certain extent by concrete behavior. Goals and behavioral acts in a firm are linked hierarchically. Division of labor within a firm is done according to a means-ends pattern. Means to reach organization goals have become subgoals which may be assigned to individual organizational units. Subgoals can be differentiated further down, until the individual job specification is reached. They are implicit or explicit in the definition of the situation as it is incorporated in the task assignment (March & Simon, 1958). Task assignments, however, are seldom–if ever–complete down to the final detail. They always leave room for personal interpretation. The signals emitted by the individual employees result from the combination of their task within the organization with their own interpretation of this task.

Many acts which perfectly fit the organization's goal structure are very job-specific. This can make the total of the signals emitted by an organization very heterogeneous. Its identity, therefore, may be homogeneous on some aspects and heterogeneous on others. Homogeneity need not be given a priori. For the purpose of corporate positioning, however, a procedure for measuring corporate identity makes more sense if it is able to filter the homogeneous elements out of the heterogeneous mass of diverse individual signals.

The characteristics (acts of behavior, goals, values) which apply to an organization as a whole are identified. The means-ends relations between these are established with the same 'laddering' technique which has been applied in the vacation study of Figure 1. This technique is based on the assumption that the respondent's acts, goals and values are related to each other in a means-ends structure, but it is in principle completely open to the content of the acts, goals and values. This way 'laddering' enables researchers to uncover characteristics which are specific to that organization and which the researchers may not have anticipated. The structuring is limited to the question "why is that important to you?," which rather triggers the respondent to provide for the structure than that the technique structures the data itself. Individual chains are aggregated and the aggregated structure is worked out in a Hierarchical Value Map, which shows how the characteristics relate to each other, and which more concrete characteristics are encompassed by which higher level characteristics.

Figure 2 presents as an example the identity of a boat company organizing excursions on the canals of Amsterdam. The more concrete actions are given at the bottom of the figure, and the upward lines show the goals at which the concrete actions are aimed. For instance, telling about the cats' boat, on the bottom line, is important because then the employee does some extra guiding. Doing some extra guiding serves the higher purpose of having personal contact, and personal contact in its turn (still following the lines upward) is important in order to provide service. Conversely, service finally takes shape among other things by telling about the cats' boat; following the lines downward Figure 2 shows how corporate goals and values are being realized through actions on the floor.

CONVEYING THE TOURIST EXPERIENCE: THE SINGLE ORGANIZATION CASE

An organization which is capable of helping tourists realize their dreams is attuned to the goals the tourist has in mind. The boat company, for instance, has the objectives of 'personal contact' and 'service.' Those goals are means for reaching (indirectly, through intermediary goals) the higher business goals such as turnover and continuity. The people in charge, including those at the more operational level, are motivated to attain these goals. If organizations working in tourism have as a goal to provide the tourist with a certain experience, ingredients of that experience should be retrieved from its Hierarchical Value Map. Figure 2 shows for instance how the employees of the boat company mix with the passengers in order to provide personal contact, how they moor the boats gently in

FIGURE 2. Hierarchical Value Map of an excursion company, organizing boat trips on the canals of Amsterdam (Source: van Rekom, 1992).

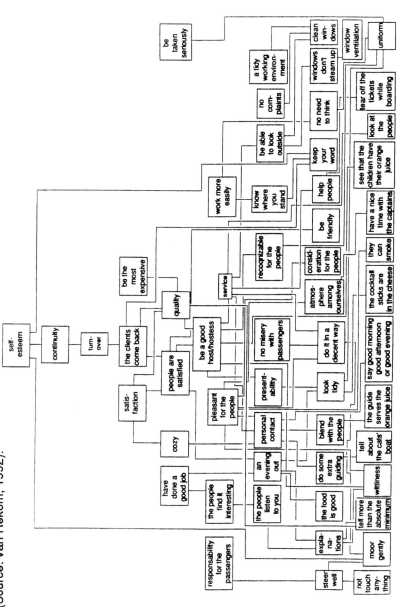

order to do it properly, and how they watch whether children have been served their orange juice in order to be a good host. If we follow the line in Figure 2 upward from that box, we see that being a good host is important in order to have satisfied clients, who will eventually come again. The employees have in mind the possibility of repeat purchases of the trip. The concrete actions are the ingredients for the clients' experience when they make a boat trip, and the Hierarchical Value Map shows, what the employees do in order to assure that experience. Of course, Figure 2 represents the perception of the people doing the job. The clients may interpret things differently. The clients' perception can be discovered via the laddering research as shown in Figure 1.

By meeting consumer choice criteria, the organization can improve the tourists' experience. In order for such a change to be effective new behavior, and perhaps new goals must therefore be incorporated into the corporate identity. Otherwise, inconsistencies between the advocated positioning and the actual way the tourist is treated will arise and the positioning may fail (van Rekom & van Riel, 1993). If an organization chooses to position on the concept 'nothing to worry about' in Figure 1, then not only the organization's communication but also the personnel on the shop floor should convey this impression.

Problems with the staff in the day-care center may spoil the whole impression of a vacation free of worries. A useful way of introducing the new behavior and goals can be established by studying the company's Hierarchical Value Map. The existing goals and values are the motivators of behavior. They will be capable of motivating the employees to adopt the new behavior, if management is able to make clear to the employees that the new behavior is an effective means of reaching the existing goals and values. Starting from the common existing values more concrete aspects to be associated with the final product can be introduced; the higher values serve as the motivation and legitimation of the internal campaign within the production chain.

A good illustration of a successful real-life application of this adage is the internal campaign of the boat excursion company in Amsterdam which is shown in Figure 2. There is one concept in the whole figure which is very central: "Being a good host/hostess." Originally, this concept did not exist at all. The guides on the boats at that time were professional guides who seemed to care more about the technical quality of the information they gave, like telling the passengers the correct years the houses were built, than about creating a pleasant atmosphere. Management wanted to change that. They wanted the clients to feel happy on board, first of all, and have them return and create a positive atmosphere of word of mouth appeal. The emphasis was to shift from technically good personnel to personnel who treated the passengers as real guests. Therefore, management set up courses, compulsory for all captains, guides and the other personnel, where everybody was taught how to be a good host–providing good service, being representative–and why it was important to be a good host: being a good host as a necessary condition to achieve quality, and to improve customer satisfaction. That is, 'being a good host' was connected to the higher level concepts of 'quality' and 'people are satisfied' (van Rekom, 1993).

AN OBSTACLE WHEN POSITIONING TRAVEL PACKAGES: THE FLEXIBILITY OF THE TOURISM PRODUCTION CHAIN

A specific aspect of tourism is that tourists generally are confronted directly with not just one, but with several members of the production chain, even if they make only one purchase decision, when they buy a package from one of the chain members. This 'end member' of the production chain can be the hotel where tourists buy a day excursion, but the more traditional example is the travel agency. The first chain member the package purchasers meet is the travel agent, when booking the trip. Then they are confronted, at the airport, with a hostess of the tour operator and during their flight with the airline personnel. Once in the country of destination, a coach company brings them to their hotel, which is again another independent member of the production chain. It might be questioned, in how far all those companies are attuned to giving the customers the 'travel experience' they have longed for. Tourists might be confronted with several totally different mentalities, instead of finding a harmonious, well balanced experience. They might be confronted with inconsistent treatment, which may have little to do with the reasons they chose this single trip out of the broad set of choice alternatives.

Each member of the chain purchases components of the package in different places. Purchasing occurs in an industrial marketing process where risks are often left to the lower members of the production chain by means of relatively short term contracts. Contracts which last only one season are not uncommon. This high flexibility of the tourism production chain as a whole makes product differentiation much more difficult; those who deliver the service of a hotel now can easily deliver this to a competitor next year. A good example is the case of Dutch incoming tourism: Large foreign tour operators may switch from one incoming agency to another, without any possibility for real differentiation, since both incoming agencies use the same coach companies, make use of a heavily overlapping network of hotels, and use the same free-lance guides. The only real benefit from changing from one agency to the other may be price. Because of the high flexibility of the chain as a whole, price is given a more prominent role for competitive advantage. In tourism, competition becomes price competition and profit margins are lower than in many other businesses–whereas sensitivity to cyclical fluctuations in the market is relatively high.

As a consequence, especially when a "complete" package is sold, a consistent product with a clear psychological value added, such as 'nothing to worry about' in Figure 1, seems difficult to develop. The special experience which is provided to the tourist, however, offers ample opportunities for differentiation. The whole production chain should be orientated to give the tourist the differentiating 'value added.' One solution is to vertically integrate the whole production chain, as has been done by the French organization Club Med. If this degree of integration is not possible, some effort should be made to accomplish a consistent mentality throughout the production chain, thereby ensuring a successful positioning and implementation of the package.

Such a mentality would set the central goals which in turn control the employees' behavior in each of the organizations participating in the tourism production chain. This means adapting their corporate identities and building a chain identity. The customers will recognize chain members by the special treatment they receive from them. 'Adapting their corporate identities' may sound quite heavy. In fact, the issue is to adopt those actions, goals and values within their own identity which allow the positioning to be successful. In a production chain for summer vacations, for the client group of Figure 1, the central goal to be adopted may be to free the clients from all kinds of possible worries. Then the corporate identities of the individual chain members will be sufficiently attuned to reaching this special end product. This end product is the 'tourist experience' which satisfies the tourists' needs and provides them with some pleasant surprises. Once the personnel of the participating organizations shares the new values, product differentiation throughout a whole production chain is possible.

CONVEYING THE DIFFERENTIATING EXPERIENCE TO THE TOURIST: BUILDING A CHAIN-LONG MENTALITY

A first step toward improvement is to measure and compare the identities of the organizations participating in a particular production chain and to look for the common denominators or aspects in the end product, which can be easily translated to common denominators. Such identity research (van Rekom, 1993) may make visible the differences which exist between the companies participating in one production chain and the tourist. A tour operator, an airline company and a hotel may have quite different associations with, for instance, the concept of 'quality.' They may also differ in their ideas about the conditions under which everything is well organized, something the respondents of Figure 1 consider important. Making the personnel of the participating organizations conscious of those differences is already an important step toward overcoming them.

The next step is to build a 'chain identity' regarding those aspects of the tourist product, which are relevant to the tourist's travel experience. Building a chain identity is not necessarily more complicated than introducing new elements in the identity of an already existing company. It does not require all organizations to become exactly alike; it does require, however, that the employees of all organizations involved are willing to contribute their ingredients into the total customer experience. Once the identities of the different chain members have been investigated, a specific internal campaign will be needed at the level of each individual organization to introduce those goals which allow the chain as a whole to realize the tourist experience. Motivation and legitimation may be different for each of them, depending upon their corporate identity. The goals which are relevant to the chain positioning are introduced as means to achieving the goals of the specific organization. Those goals are chosen which best suit the desired behavior. Although the employees of the participating organizations may be convinced with different arguments, the end result will be a common goal orientation for the whole production chain, which matches the relevant part of the goals of the target tourist group. If, for instance, a particular production chain develops as its common goal to give the tourists the feeling, that 'there is nothing to worry about,' the employees have to be convinced in terms of their own value system as to why this common goal is important. Each of them can perform the actions which lie within his own role in order to realize the common goal. Once the personnel of all the companies participating in a package shares those differentiating values and goals, the tourists can really undergo the experience they long for when buying the package, in this example the vacation, free of all kind of worries. Then the tourist product really obtains an added psychological value.

Common sharing of those goals and values should result in behavior which contributes to their realization, and tourists are consistently helped in achieving their expectations. Common points of departure for the corporate communication (van Riel, 1994) are well defined and translated into concrete actions by all employees of all companies involved. Essentially this is the same principle which is operating in a symphony orchestra. All musicians, as well as the director and the technical assistants, have to be fully aware of the emotional meaning of the performance and moreover, they have to feel the urge to give the emotional meaning of the symphony being played its full splendor. A symphony performance in this way is very much like a 'vacation performance.'

Once a group of partners working together toward the implementation of a 'package deal' has reached this stage, successful product differentiation will be possible. The product itself will become the focus of the competition, not the price. Working effectively on the realization of their clients' dreams, tourism as a business could be able to escape from the vicious circle of price competition and low profit margins.

CONCLUSION

Tourism offers the consumer a non-ordinary experience. One of the most central tourist motives is the 'escape' notion. Escape, basically, is the search for gratification of those human needs which are not fulfilled in daily life. In order to know how tourists try to fulfill their needs, we need to know how their travel choices relate to their goals and values. The 'laddering' technique is a research technique very well suited to that purpose. Starting from specific choice criteria, it is able to uncover the more constant goals, which control the more concrete choice criteria, and which provide for a sound basis for possible positioning strategies. But then the promised expectations still need to be met. An organization which is able to help tourists realize their dreams should be attuned to realizing the goals the tourist has in mind. Direct interactions on the shop floor are the ingredients for the client's experience. If new activities have to be introduced for this purpose, the existing goals and values can fulfill the function of motivating the employees to adopt the new behavior–provided it can be made clear to them that the new behavior is an effective means of attaining the existing goals.

In general, however, the tourist is directly confronted with several suppliers in the tourism production chain. The whole production chain should be oriented to give the tourist the differentiating 'added value.' Some effort will be required to build a chain-long mentality. If the chain members differ in mentality, at each individual organization a specific internal campaign will be needed to introduce those goals which will allow the chain as a whole to realize the tourist's experience. The goals which are relevant to the chain positioning are introduced as means to the goals living in the specific organizations. Once the personnel of all participating companies share those differentiating values and goals, tourists can really undergo the experience that the end member in the production chain sells them. Then the tourist product obtains a psychological added value, and successful product differentiation will be possible.

REFERENCES

Braun, O.L., and M. Lohman (1989). *Die Reiseentscheidung; einige Ergebnisse zum Stand der Forschung.* Schriftenreihe für Tourismusforschung. Studienkreis für Tourismus e.V., Starnberg.

Calantone, R., and J.A. Mazanec (1991). Marketing Management and Tourism. *Annals of Tourism Research*, vol. 18, N° 1: 101-119.

Iso-Ahola, S.E. (1984). Social Psychological Foundations of Leisure and Resultant Implications for Leisure Counseling. In: E.T. Dowd (ed.): *Leisure Counseling: Concepts and Applications*, 97-125. Springfield, IL: Charles C Thomas.

Jafari, J. and R.M. Gardner (1991). *Tourism and Fiction; Travel as a fiction–fiction as a journey.* Cahiers du Tourisme, Série C, N° 119. Centre des Hautes Études Touristiques, Aix-en-Provence, France.

Kaspar, C. (1989). The significance of Enterprise Culture for Tourism Enterprises. *Revue de Tourisme, 3*, 2-4.

Liebman Parrinello, G. (1993). Motivation and Anticipation in Post-Industrial Tourism. *Annals of Tourism Research, 20*, 233-249.

Mannell, R.C. and S.E. Iso-Ahola (1987). Psychological Nature of Leisure and Tourism Experience. *Annals of Tourism Research, 14*, 314-331.

March, J.G. and H.A. Simon. 1958. *Organizations.* New York: John Wiley.

Olson, J.C. and T.J. Reynolds (1984). Understanding Consumers' Cognitive Structures: Implications for Advertising Strategy. In: L. Percy and A.G. Woodside (eds.): *Advertising and Consumer Psychology*. Lexington, MA: Lexington Books, 77-90.

Pieters, R. (1993). A Control View on the Behavior of Consumers: Turning the Triangle. In: W.F. van Raaij and G. Bamossy (eds.): *European Advances in Consumer Research*, Vol. 1, 507-512.

Pitts, R.E. and A.G. Woodside (1986). Personal Values and Travel Decisions. *Journal of Travel Research*, 25, N° 1, 20-25.

Reynolds, Th.J. and J. Gutman. (1984). Advertising is Image Management. *Journal of Advertising Research*. February/March 1984, *24*, 27-36.

Robie, C., A.G. Bateson, P.A. Ellison and M.H. Figler (1993). An Analysis of the Tourism Motivation Construct. *Annals of Tourism Research, 20*, 773-776.

van Raaij, W. F., and D.A. Francken (1984). Vacation Decisions, Activities and Satisfactions. *Annals of Tourism Research, 11*, 101-112.

van Rekom, J. (1992). Corporate Identity; Ontwikkeling van Concept en Meetinstrument. [Corporate Identity: Development of Concept and Measuring Instrument] In: C.B.M. van Riel & W.H. Nijhof (eds.): *Handboek Corporate Communication*. Houten, Van Loghum Slaterus.

van Rekom, J. (1993). Measuring Corporate Identity–Its measurement and use in Corporate Communication. *Proceedings of the 22nd Annual Conference of the European Marketing Academy*, pp. 1497-1514. ESADE, Barcelona.

van Rekom, J., and C.B.M. van Riel (1993). Corporate Communication van Geïntegreerde Communicatie naar Integrerende Communicatie [Corporate Communication; from integrated communication toward integrating communication], *Bedrijfskunde*, 1993, nr. 2, 157-171.

van Riel, C.B.M. (1994). *An introduction into Corporate Communication Theory*. Hemel Hempstead: Prentice Hall. (in press)

Witt, C.A. and P.L. Wright (1991). Tourist Motivation: Life after Maslow. In: P. Johnson and B. Thomas: *Choice and Demand in Tourism*. London: Mansell Publishing Limited.

Consumer Behavior and Tourism: Review and Extension of Four Study Areas

Frédéric Dimanche
Mark E. Havitz

SUMMARY. Consumer behavior research constitutes a cornerstone of marketing strategy and practice, and an increasing number of tourist behavior studies have been published in the past few years. This paper examines the current literature related to four prevalent topical areas associated with consumer behavior in recreational and touristic contexts: Ego involvement, loyalty and commitment, family decision-making, and novelty seeking. The paper's primary focus is on conceptual and measurement issues, but implications of each of these areas to marketing practice are also considered.

Solomon (1992) defined consumer behavior as the study of the processes involved when individuals or groups select, purchase, use, or dispose of products, services, ideas, or experiences to satisfy needs and desires. Van Raaij (1986, p. 2) posited that "Consumer research on tourism should be a cornerstone of marketing strategy." Indeed, an understanding of consumer behavior is required in order to make adequate

Frédéric Dimanche is affiliated with the School of Hotel, Restaurant and Tourism Administration, College of Business, University of New Orleans, New Orleans, LA 70148.

Mark E. Havitz is affiliated with the Department of Recreation and Leisure Studies, University of Waterloo.

[Haworth co-indexing entry note]: "Consumer Behavior and Tourism: Review and Extension of Four Study Areas." Dimanche, Frédéric, and Mark E. Havitz. Co-published simultaneously in the *Journal of Travel & Tourism Marketing* (The Haworth Press, Inc.) Vol. 3, No. 3, 1994, pp. 37-57; and: *Economic Psychology of Travel and Tourism* (ed: John C. Crotts, and W. Fred van Raaij), The Haworth Press, Inc., 1994, pp. 37-57. Multiple copies of this article/chapter may be purchased from The Haworth Document Delivery Center [1-800-3-HAWORTH; 9:00 a.m. - 5:00 p.m. (EST)].

marketing decisions (Moutinho, 1987). Typically, consumer behavior has attempted to explain the decision making processes of consumers facing several alternatives or choices. Consumer behavior research has attained increasing prominence in the leisure literature in the past decade, but relatively few tourist-based consumer behavior studies have been conducted in the past years, with some exceptions such as satisfaction and motivation research (e.g., Crompton, 1979; Dann, 1981; Mansfeld, 1992; van Raaij & Francken, 1984). A large segment of academic research is dedicated to tourism marketing, and it seems that more studies have focused on describing or segmenting tourists rather than understanding and explaining their consumption behavior. The tourism experience, although unique because of its nature, can be related to consumption behavior (Dimanche & Samdahl, 1991; Urry, 1990), and specific studies examining the interactions between the many elements and processes involved in consumer behavior should be conducted in the context of tourism.

The purpose of this paper is to review and synthesize current literature related to four topical areas associated with consumer behavior in recreational and touristic contexts: Ego involvement, loyalty and commitment, family decision-making, and novelty seeking. The implications of each of these areas to marketing practice will also be considered although this paper's primary focus will be on conceptual and measurement issues. These four topics do not represent the breadth of all consumer behavior research, nor are they necessarily the highest priority area for future study. However, they have been well covered in the consumer behavior and marketing literature and have recently received growing attention in the travel and leisure literature. Because of their intrinsic importance in the tourist's decision-making process, each shows promise for better understanding recreational and touristic behavior. With regards to involvement theory, Stewart and Stynes have contributed to this edition with a paper titled "Toward a dynamic model of complex tourism choices: The seasonal home location decision." Also, Gitelson and Kerstetter added to this edition's treatment of family decision-making with their article on "The influence of non-family members in travel decision making."

EGO INVOLVEMENT

Among these four topics, the largest body of leisure and tourism research is related to involvement. Consumer involvement with products has been the object of a long line of research in the consumer behavior literature, and it is now widely recognized as a significant variable by marketing scholars and practitioners. The following will outline the state of involvement research in touristic and recreational contexts and indicate recommendations for future studies (a selection of major findings related to involvement in tourism and leisure contexts appears in Table 1).

Involvement can be defined as an unobservable state of motivation, arousal, or interest, evoked by a particular stimulus or situation, and that has drive properties. Its consequences are types of searching, information-processing, and decision making (Rothschild, 1984). Most of the involvement research in leisure and tourism contexts has initially focused on conceptual and measurement concerns (e.g., Dimanche, Havitz, & Howard, 1991; Havitz & Dimanche, 1990; McIntyre, 1989; Selin & Howard, 1988; Watkins, 1987). These conceptual and methodological studies paved the way for considering involvement as a multidimensional construct. Most involvement researchers (e.g., Dimanche et al., 1991; Laurent & Kapferer, 1985; McIntyre & Pigram, 1992; McQuarrie & Munson, 1987) agree that multi-

TABLE 1. Selected leisure and tourism-related research with involvement (inv.).

Authors and dates	Purpose or findings
Selin & Howard (1988)	Conceptual presentation of inv. to explain attachment between individuals and leisure pursuits.
Bloch et al. (1989)	Sport equipment inv. found to significantly influence spending levels and opinion leadership.
Fesenmaier & Johnson (1989)	Behavioral measure of inv. found useful to segment tourists.
McIntyre (1989)	Empirical study showing the multidimensional nature of inv.
Havitz & Dimanche (1990)	Conceptual argument and propositions for using multidimensional inv. in leisure and tourism studies.
Dimanche et al. (1991)	Translated Inv. Profile scale and tested its validity and reliability in recreational and touristic contexts.
Norman (1991)	Inv. and previous vacation experience better predictor of travel intentions than other psychological variables.
Madrigal et al. (1992)	Relationships between level of inv. with family vacations and selected personal variables were found.
McIntyre & Pigram (1992)	used inv. profiles to differentiate between campers.
Dimanche et al. (1993)	Inv. profiles shown useful as tourism segmentation tool.
Reid & Crompton (1993)	Conceptual argument and propositions for studying involvement's relationships to 5 decision-making paradigms.

dimensional conceptualizations which consider antecedent dimensions of the construct are more accurate and useful than simple high-low involvement distinctions. For further review of the involvement construct in the consumer behavior literature, the reader is referred to Laurent and Kapferer (1985) and Zaichkowsky (1985). Most consumer behavior research has been conducted in product contexts, whereas recreation and tourism research has focused more on activity contexts.

Dimanche et al. (1991) translated from French, then tested for reliability and validity the Involvement Profile (IP) scale (Laurent & Kapferer, 1985). This scale, designed to measure four facets of involvement (i.e., importance-pleasure, sign value,[1] risk consequences, and risk probability) in recreational and touristic contexts, was subsequently used in studies of activities where involvement was either a dependent or an independent variable. For example, Dimanche, Havitz, and Howard (1993) showed that involvement could be used in touristic contexts as a basis for market segmentation, responding to Fesenmaier and Johnson's (1989), and Havitz and Dimanche's (1990) recommendations. Their segmentation study demonstrated that involvement profiles, revealing the facets of involvement, provided more information about a person's relationship to a touristic activity than a single involvement score. Dimanche et al. (1993) noted that the practical application of involvement segmentation extends well beyond promotional implications to program development, pricing, and distribution strategies.

A future challenge for involvement researchers will be to measure tourists' involvement with destinations. Measuring people's involvement profiles with various vacation destinations would have relevance for businesses such as airlines, tour-operators, travel agencies, or for organizations such as conventions and visitors bureaux, state or national tourism agencies, etc.

At least two directions of tourism destination involvement research have been suggested to date. Brown (1991) explored tourism place-identity from the perspective of guests (tourists), whereas Ap (1992) examined destination involvement from the perspective of hosts (local residents). Both directions offer promise for improving the quality of experiences for both host and guest populations, and they also allow for tests of theory. Brown's symbolic interaction-based inquiry was qualitative and did not utilize any of the standardized instrumentation common to much of the research cited in this section. However, specific facets of involvement such as importance and sign (Havitz & Dimanche, 1990) were central to tourists' descriptions of place. Also, Ap found that destination involvement was an important component of the social exchange model developed to study host-guest relations.

Another potentially important area of research that has been neglected by consumer behavior researchers and which could make a significant contribution to tourism marketing is the study of consumer involvement with services. To date, involvement researchers' focus has been on products and activities, despite the economic importance of the service sector, and the distinction between products and services (Zeithaml, Parasuraman, & Berry, 1985). Celuch and Longfellow (1992) used a multidimensional conceptualization of involvement to initiate this line of research in the context of services such as life insurance, medical services, or restaurants. Tourism researchers certainly should further develop the study of tourist involvement with touristic services.

Researchers continue to explore the relationship between enduring and situational involvement (Howard & Havitz, 1993; Richins, Bloch, & McQuarrie, 1992), as well as the importance of involvement in pricing, communication (advertising and promotion), and product development strategies. Richins et al. found that the relationship between situational and enduring (ego) involvement was better described by an additive model rather than an interactive model. That is, situational involvement did not increase or decrease exponentially based on individuals' levels of enduring involvement. Rather, situational and enduring components seemed to operate relatively independent of each other, both contributing to overall involvement with purchase decisions. Howard and Havitz found general support for Laurent and Kapferer's (1985) conceptual argument that importance and pleasure represent enduring facets and that sign and risk consequences fluctuate based on situational considerations. In this case the situational contexts were represented by in-season, off-season, and pre-season measurements of involvement with golfing, skiing, and windsurfing. Contrary to predictions, scores appeared to be stable (enduring) across seasons for the risk probability facet.

Involvement is generally acknowledged in the consumer behavior literature as a major factor in the decision making process; therefore, exploring the relationships between the involvement facets and specific behaviors such as information search, receptivity to promotional stimuli, or brand loyalty should be tourism researchers' next priority. For example, researchers could explore how to increase tourists' levels of involvement with destinations or tourism services. An involved consumer is more likely to understand and memorize promotional stimuli, and to purchase the product or service that raised his/her level of involvement. Though none have been conducted to date, numerous opportunities for controlled experimental studies exist in this area. The relationship between involvement and perceptions of service quality should also be examined as has been done with loyalty research (Veldkamp & Backman, 1992) and complaint behavior research (Twynam, 1993). The study of service quality became more sophisticated with the development of standardized measurement tools resulting from the pioneering efforts of Parasuraman, Zeithaml, and Berry (1985, 1988). The nature of the relationship between involvement and perceptions of service quality appears to be an area needing exploration. For example, high involvement services may have different service quality definitions than low involvement services. Specific relationships could be found between the facets of involvement and the dimensions of service quality. Better comprehension of these constructs could help marketers understand their role in the formation of purchase intentions. Although service quality–involvement linkages are yet to be explored, researchers have begun to link involvement research with other social-psychological constructs.

Norman (1991) indicated that level of involvement and previous vacation experience were better predictors of summer travel than were other social psychological variables. Also, the effect of involvement can be related to consumer loyalty towards services. Pritchard (1992) found that involvement levels were positively correlated to psychological commitment with hotels and airlines. Siegenthaler and Lam (1992) found similar results in the context of recreational tennis. These results were consistent with Backman and Crompton's (1990a, 1990b) findings that level of involvement and attitude toward recreational activities such as tennis and golf were the best predictors of whether people would drop-out or continue participation. Madrigal, Havitz, and Howard's (1992) study of married couples' family vacation decision processes reveal relationships between involvement and gender role ideology. Specifically, more modern couples found the process to be more important and pleasurable than did more traditional couples.

The measurement tools to study involvement have been developed. Researchers now need to focus on understanding the relationships between involvement and other constructs in order to provide tourism marketers with practical recommendations that will enhance the tourist's experience.

LOYALTY AND COMMITMENT

Loyalty represents another construct central to the study of tourist behavior. Service providers (e.g., airlines or hotels) rival with strategies such as frequent user programs in order to create customer loyalty. It is a well-known fact to marketers that keeping customers is less expensive than creating new ones. The challenge is to understand and appropriately use the factors that will determine customer loyalty (a selection of significant loyalty research in tourism and leisure contexts appears in Table 2).

Similarly to involvement, measurement and conceptual issues have dominated research related to loyalty and commitment (Buchanan, 1985). Day (1969, p. 35) argued that loyalty was based on an evaluative decision and affective orientation which could be considered a "commitment to the brand." This close association characterized most early research which generally did not distinguish between loyalty and commitment. Pritchard, Howard, and Havitz (1992) noted that loyalty and commitment represent but two of the numerous terms in this line of research. An additional

TABLE 2. Selected leisure and tourism-related research with loyalty and commitment.

Authors and dates	Purpose or findings
Jarvis & Mayo (1986)	Developed a two-dimensional (attitudes and frequency of stay) paradigm of hotel loyalty. Seven loyalty types are described
Gyte & Phelps (1989)	Investigated the pattern of repeat visitation to a vacation destination.
Backman & Crompton (1990a)	Developed a two-dimensional (psychological attachment and behavioral consistency) paradigm of activity loyalty. Four types are described (i.e., low, spurious, latent, and high).
Backman & Crompton (1990b)	Behavioral, attitudinal, and composite measures of activity loyalty capture three different dimensions of the phenomenon.
Pritchard et al. (1992)	Review of commitment and loyalty literature.
Pritchard (1992)	Developed and tested an instrument to measure tourist loyalty. Correlation between inv.and commitment to hotels and airlines were found.
Twynam (1992)	Support found for Singh's model of consumer complaint behavior in travel contexts. Various dimensions of inv. were correlated with propensity to complain about poor service, and with alternative courses of action.
Pritchard & Howard (1993)	Argued that traditional unidimensional measurement of the attitudinal component of loyalty is incomplete. Developed the PCI which measures symbolic consistency, volition, and complexity.

problem was early researchers' inconsistent and interchangeable use of attitudinal and behavioral measures of loyalty. This confusion was partially clarified when Backman and Crompton (1990a, 1990b) and Jarvis and Mayo (1986) proposed two-dimensional typologies for considering attitudinal and behavioral components of loyalty in recreational activities and travel contexts, respectively. These two-dimensional conceptualizations greatly enhanced our understanding of consumer loyalty. They are not without shortcomings however. For example, Pritchard et al. (1992) provided evidence that both the behavioral and attitudinal components are very complex (i.e., multidimensional) and that numerous measurement options are available. Four types of behavioral loyalty measurement have been commonly used in consumer research: Sequence of brand purchase, proportion of brand purchase, probability of purchase, and combinations of the first three measures (Jacoby & Chestnut, 1978). Pritchard's (1992) research suggested that the latter form of measurement is most appropriate in tourism contexts because behavioral loyalty patterns varied widely based on industry types (i.e., lodging, transportation, and attractions). As such, results of even relatively simple behavioral loyalty research are often difficult to compare directly.

The attitudinal component is even more complex and as a result is often ignored in loyalty research or more subject to ad hoc measurement. Pritchard et al. (1992) argued that loyalty and commitment are not interchangeable terms and that commitment should be reserved only for the attitudinal component of loyalty. Pritchard and Howard's (1993) Psychological Commitment Instrument (PCI) provided the first rigorous measure of tourist commitment. The PCI was subjected to a rigorous battery of reliability and validity tests yielding a three-dimensional instrument which measures: (a) symbolic consistency, respondents' overall reluctance to change important associations; (b) respondents' perceptions of complexity, the number of ideas or reasons impacting the decision; and (c) their perceptions of volition, or the component of free choice and control over their preferences. Pritchard tested the PCI in the context of transportation services, hospitality services, and attraction oriented services, in order to ensure that the instrument would be applicable to the broadest possible range of travel services.

The conceptual and measurement advances made by Backman and Crompton (1990a; 1990b), Buchanan (1985), Jarvis and Mayo (1986), and Pritchard (1992) should pay dividends in the near future. These advances should be especially helpful in clarifying the relationship between loyalty and other social-psychological constructs such as involvement and perception of service quality. Numerous exploratory efforts have been undertaken in the past few years. For example, Twynam (1993) studied the relationship between complaint behavior and loyalty, and found that dissatisfied travelers used a complex mix of voice (seek redress from the seller), private (negative word of mouth), and third party (e.g., legal action) responses. Hotel patrons were much more likely to switch brands than were airline patrons. Bloch, Black, and Lichtenstein (1989) and Siegenthaler and Lam (1992) examined the relationship between commitment and ego involvement. Bloch et al. found no significant relationship between equipment involvement and behavioral commitment (loyalty), whereas Siegenthaler and Lam found a positive relationship between activity involvement and attitudinal commitment. Backman (1991) found no relationship between social, individual, and price constraints in leisure loyalty. However, transportation- and promotion-related constraints were perceived differently by people in various loyalty-based segments. Veldkamp and Backman (1992) recorded that participants' perceptions of the importance of the tangible dimensions of service quality was related to loyalty types. However, other dimensions of service quality were not related to them. In summary, leisure researchers have established tentative relationships between loyalty and other social-psychological constructs. Nevertheless, few of these studies were conducted in tourism contexts and multiple instruments were used to measure each construct. For example, involvement was measured in three of those studies, each time with a different scale. Replication and extension of these exploratory efforts are needed before definitive conclusions can be established.

NOVELTY

The concept of novelty seeking is not new or should we say, not novel to tourism researchers. Not surprisingly, of the four consumer behavior topics discussed in this paper, novelty is the one area that is more prevalent in tourism research than in leisure research. Three decades ago, psychologists such as Berlyne (1960) and Hunt (1961) studied people's search for incongruity, uncertainty, novelty and complexity. Theoretically, novelty or the discontinuation of routine leads to higher levels of arousal, and tourists may seek experiences that provide new sources of stimulation. Novelty seeking is often reported as a key motive in tourist motivation studies (e.g., Crompton, 1979; Dann, 1981). The literature also seems to indicate that "vacationers taking novel trips differ in several fundamental ways from vacationers taking familiar or common place trips" (Bello & Etzel, 1985). For example, vacationers taking novel trips seek more advice on the destination and spend more time and money during the trip than do travelers taking commonplace trips (a selection of novelty-related research in tourism contexts appears in Table 3).

Two decades ago, Cohen (1972) and Plog (1974) presented novelty-oriented tourism typologies based on sociological and psychological models respectively. Initially accepted with little challenge, these two widely cited typologies have formed the conceptual basis for much of the recently conducted tourism novelty research. Cohen (1972) tried to differentiate between international tourists based on the degree to which they seek novelty or familiarity in their travel experience, originally proposing four tourist roles: "drifter," "explorer," "individual mass tourist," and "organized mass tourist." He then recommended (1974) that further methodological refinement be used to measure these differences in quantitative terms. Pearce (1985) noted that unfortunately, researchers were slow to follow Cohen's suggestion.

Snepenger (1987) conducted the first empirical test of Cohen's typology using Cohen's roles to segment travelers to Alaska and found partial support for the typology. Three of Cohen's four original tourist roles were evident in the sample: organized mass tourist (54% of the sample), individual mass tourist (20%), and explorer (26%). However, three limitations of Snepenger's work have been pointed out. First, the study only consid-

TABLE 3. Selected leisure and tourism-related research with novelty.

Authors and dates	Purpose or findings
Cohen (1972)	Conceptual classification of international tourist roles based on novelty seeking.
Bello & Etzel (1985)	Novelty seekers' behavior differ from familiarity seekers.
Snepenger (1987)	Found some support for Cohen's typology, using a behavioral measure of loyalty.
Yiannakis & Gibson (1992)	Developed and tested a Travel Role Preference Questionnaire.
Lee & Crompton (1992)	Developed and tested a four-dimensional scale measuring novelty seeking.
Crotts (1993)	Investigated correlations between novelty seeking (measured with behavior) and personality.
Reinecke, Flynn & Goldsmith (1993)	Tested a one-dimensional innovativeness scale in the context of travel services
Mo et al. (1993)	Developed and tested a three-dimensional International Tourist Role scale.

ered the behavioral component of novelty, admittedly also an attitudinal construct. Second, a single item was used to operationalize behavior, and third the sample frame included primarily domestic rather than international tourists.

In contrast to the relatively ad hoc nature of most previous quantitative novelty-based instrumentation, Yiannakis and Gibson (1992) developed their Travel Role Preference Questionnaire (TRPQ) with an extensive battery of reliability and validity tests. Their research has advanced considerably researchers' abilities to operationalize the various forms of touristic behavior described in Cohen's (1979) and Pearce's (1982, 1985) work. Yiannakis and Gibson tested the TRPQ with several probability and purposively selected samples and reported 13 distinct tourist roles, a more discriminating set of roles than was reported in either Cohen's early (1972) or latter (1974) efforts. Respondents are asked to consider TRPQ items based on "the degree to which a variety of roles best described their actual behaviors while on vacation" (p. 292).

Another recent advance, Mo, Howard, and Havitz' (1993) 20-item International Tourist Role (ITR) scale was designed to capture the novelty related nuances of international pleasure travel as proposed by Cohen (1972). Like the TRPQ, it was subjected to a rigorous battery of reliability and validity tests. The items comprising the ITR scale represent three dimensions. The "Destination-Oriented Dimension" (DOD) represents an individual's preferences for novelty and familiarity especially when choosing among international travel destinations. The "Travel Services Dimension" (TSD) measures the extent to which an individual prefers to travel with or without institutionalized travel services when traveling in a foreign country. The "Social Contact Dimension" (SCD) measures the individual's preferences regarding the extent and variety of social contacts with local people when traveling in a foreign country. Practical application of the ITR scale suggested that it is effective in generating distinct target markets based on novelty seeking attitudes and that the target markets are also socio-demographically and behaviorally distinct (Mo et al., 1993).

The travel preference groups identified by Mo et al. (1993) and Yiannakis and Gibson (1992) share characteristics with, but are not identical to the original four groups proposed by Cohen. For example, Mo et al. reported a universally novelty seeking group (similar to Cohen's drifters) and a universally familiarity seeking group (similar to Cohen's organized mass tourist). But, they also reported several groups with complex novelty seeking preferences that were not analogous to Cohen's middle range (individual mass tourist and explorer) groups. Therefore, the tourist roles described in the two recent studies may be different from Cohen's original roles because of the more complex multidimensional interpretation of novelty. Cohen's typology is not wrong, but it may oversimplify the reality of tourist roles. Extensions on the original model were also expressed in Cohen's most recent work.

Another rigorously tested novelty seeking scale was developed by Lee and Crompton (1992). Purporting to measure the psychological construct of novelty, this scale comprised four dimensions: thrill, change from routine, boredom alleviation, and surprise. Lee and Crompton confirmed that tourists could be differentiated on the basis of novelty seeking attitudes. Their review of the novelty seeking phenomenon was more comprehensive in scope than was the work of Yiannakis and Gibson (1992) and Mo et al. (1993) who focused primarily on the theoretical works of Cohen (1972) and Pearce (1985). In this sense, Lee and Crompton's scale may have the broadest application potential of the three scales whereas the TRPQ and ITR scales may provide more in-depth information in specific circumstances. Rather than competing with each other, these three scales may be complementary because they were not designed to serve the same purpose. For example, The ITR and TRPQ scales, which were developed in the context of international tourism may find some applications with marketers concerned with attracting international tourists, whereas Lee and Crompton's scale may be used with either international or domestic travelers, and perhaps even in non-touristic leisure contexts. The ITR can be used to study attitudes of experienced international travelers and people who have not traveled internationally whereas the TRPQ assumes some past travel experience.

All three scales were developed in English using American samples. Therefore, their use with markets from other countries and cultures may be limited at this point. Dimanche (in press) and Plog (1991) highlighted the special challenges associated with conducting multicultural research in tourism situations. Nonetheless, the novelty topic and the growth of international travel combine to provide a fertile area for future research. Expanded research agendas using all three of these scales with a variety of international samples represent a logical next step.

Pragmatically, knowledge of the novelty construct can be used by destination marketers who may want to use in their communication strategies some cues that would attract novelty seekers or, in the opposite, familiarity seekers. Less apparent, but equally if not more important, novelty research can help tourism planners develop appropriate facilities and programs, distribution, and pricing strategies that are congruent with the benefits sought by specific markets.

Like Cohen's work, Plog's (1974) typology has also been widely cited.

However, academicians have been slow to apply it and test it. Plog posited that the members of the US population could be classified on a psychographic continuum. At one extreme are psychocentrics, whose concerns are self-centered and relatively narrow. At the other end are allocentrics, whose concerns and interests are varied in nature. Plog (1991) argued that this typology may be helpful in determining an individual's propensity to travel, the type of travel services used, and the type of destinations they would select. His 1974 work suggested that the typology was most accurate in classifying individuals near the poles and less accurate for classifying individuals in between (midcentrics).

Smith (1990a) authored the first independent test of the allocentric-psychocentric typology using international travel markets. He found very limited support for the typology as a predictor of travel destination choice. Following that, Plog (1991) and Smith (1990b) published a series of exchanges in which they clarified their positions regarding the legitimacy of Smith's independent test. More recently, Madrigal's (1993) research also showed limited support for the typology. Using the five-item instrument developed by Plog, Madrigal found some relationship between personality measures (allocentrism and psychocentrism) and personal values as measured with Kahle and Timmer's (1983) List of Values (LOV) scale. However, the personality measures did not differentiate between package group and independent travelers whereas the higher order personal values scores did differentiate between traveler types. Madrigal's dependent variable (travel type) was distinct from Smith's dependent variable (travel destination) although both represent questions addressed in Plog's (1974) research.

Based on Smith's and Madrigal's work, Plog's personality measure has not received the level of empirical support found for the sociological model proposed by Cohen. However, it is apparent that many avenues of novelty research remain untapped and it would be premature to pass final judgement based on so few data sets.

FAMILY DECISION MAKING

The issue of family decision making should also be of interest to marketers. In fact, most consumer behavior texts devote an entire chapter to the topic. Nevertheless, family decision making has received relatively little attention by leisure and tourism researchers. Much of the family research published in the leisure literature has focused on the impact of leisure activity on family interaction and cohesion (Orthner & Mancini, 1990), gender roles, and on perceptions of fun and work (Shaw, 1992).

Leisure serves as an independent variable in this type of research. In contrast, a primary contribution of consumer researchers is to conduct research in which leisure (including leisure travel) is the dependent variable and variables such as gender role and involvement become independent variables. This type of research is vitally important. For example, knowing who makes the decision about travel destinations in a household, and which family members influence this decision could contribute greatly to the effectiveness of communication strategies and other marketing decisions (a selection of family decision-making research appears in Table 4). Jenkins' (1978) early work provided evidence of dominance by some spouses in travel decision-making. Changing lifestyles and increasing participation of women in the work force may alter family decision-making processes, and therefore, these processes should be monitored and better understood (Nichols & Snepenger, 1988). Family life cycle stages are also thought to be influential in the decision process. For example, Cosenza and Davis (1981) indicated that to each step in the life cycle corresponded a specific dominance type in the couple's decision making process. Also related to family life cycle stages is the importance of the children. Jenkins noted their influence on sub-decisions in traveling contexts. Industry researchers are now paying more attention to children and teenagers than ever before. Not only are children and teens future paying customers, but many already possess some discretionary income, and their role as a market of influencers is now recognized (Neal, 1992). In tourism contexts, an increasing number of communication strategies are now targeting children directly, or parents with children. The need for better understanding children's influence in travel decisions should justify further research in that area.

Early travel related family research tended to focus on husband and wife's (and to a lesser extent, children's) decision making roles (Filiatrault & Ritchie, 1980; Myers & Moncrief, 1978; Nichols & Snepenger, 1988). The consensus of these studies suggested that joint decisions were more common than husband dominant or wife dominant decisions. The target marketing and marketing mix implications of such research are generally quite straightforward although they can be complicated by issues such as changing gender norms and family roles over time. To date, no longitudinal data have ever been collected on this topic. More recently, Madrigal (1990) found that although most decisions were shared, issue salience, gender role ideology, and personal resources of various actors also affected decisions. Building on that research, Madrigal et al. (1992) found relationships between several facets of involvement, gender role ideology, and sociodemographic characteristics.

TABLE 4. Selected leisure and tourism-related research with family decision-making (DM).

Authors and dates	Purpose or findings
Jenkins (1978)	Found evidence of some spouse dominance dependent on sub-decisions. Influence of children recognized.
Cosenza & Davis (1981)	Influence and decision structures varied across stages of the family life cycle.
Nichols & Snepenger (1988)	Joint DM couples had different DM processes than did one-spouse dominant couples.
Neal (1992)	The importance of children as an "influence" market is stressed
Madrigal (1992)	Issue salience was a significant predictor of vacation DM among married couples. Couples with traditional gender roles ideologies exhibited different DM processes from couples with modern gender role ideology.
Shaw (1992)	Time-budget and interview-based methods revealed difference in perceptions of work and leisure components of family based leisure. Women were more likely to perceive family time as work when compared with the perceptions of men.

An interesting challenge faced by family researchers relates to the collection and interpretation of data from multiple individuals (e.g, dyads, triads) rather than from individual subjects. Howard and Madrigal (1990) acknowledged these difficulties in an exploratory study in which respondents (primarily mothers) were asked to judge the perceptions of other family members regarding purchase decisions for recreation services. Madrigal's (1991) exploration of married couples' family vacation decisions used a more sophisticated dyadic approach.

METHODOLOGICAL RECOMMENDATIONS

Research discussed in this paper is dominated by survey methodology and at least two alternative methodologies have potential to contribute to future consumer behavior investigations. Some of the questions that remain to be asked demand different methodological approaches. For example, Shaw (1992) provided convincing evidence of the utility of qualitative techniques when researching family decisions. Indeed, qualitative methodologies should not be ignored for studying any of the four topics discussed in this paper. Much of the conceptual work supporting theory development in these areas has been conducted using qualitative methodologies. The Experience Sampling Method (ESM) which has gained prominence among leisure behaviorists (e.g., Samdahl, 1988) may also provide a promising tool for studying family decision making. This technique consists of providing respondents with an electronic pager and a block of self report forms with open-ended and scaled items. Respondents are then paged at random times throughout the day, and information on moods, feelings, and activities are collected at those times. Open-ended questioning and in-depth interviews could contribute to understanding the various meanings of risk and the directionality of sign value (positive or negative) in involvement. For example, data collected using the IP scale may indicate that taking a cruise says something about the respondents. We need to further investigate with interviews whether those perceptions of sign value are positive or negative. Another benefit of some qualitative research methods such as in-depth interviews is that they provide opportunities for reciprocal benefits to participants. Participants immediately gain insight into their own behaviors, attitudes, or motivations. In contrast, in most studies, individual results are rarely communicated to respondents.

Similarly, survey data are inadequate for understanding the relationship between mediating variables such as involvement and commitment, and outcomes such as decision-making, purchase behavior, or participation patterns. Controlled laboratory experiments and field experiments provide better opportunities for responding to such research questions. Finally, all four constructs discussed in this paper must be understood in relation to time. However, most studies conducted to date have measured the construct at one point in time. Therefore, future research agendas should include longitudinal methods such as time series, or panel survey methods where multiple data sets are collected over time.

CONCLUSION

This paper presented four topics related to the study of tourist behavior which are showing great promise for better understanding the consumption of tourism, as well as for contributing to the practice of tourism marketing. As the industry matures and becomes increasingly competitive, successful marketing practices must be based on a solid knowledge of consumer behavior. Our growing comprehension of tourist behavior will likely shed some light on the consumption of tourism and travel services, and the mechanisms that underlie the economics of destinations. Research on involvement, loyalty-commitment, novelty, and family decision-making has been more exploratory than confirmatory. As a group, consumer researchers have largely avoided the temptation to answer practical questions without adequate conceptualization and without the benefit of reliable and valid instrumentation. This is especially characteristic of much of the research published in the last five years. Consequently, many of the recent studies are long on internal validity and short on external validity. Future academic and applied studies should benefit from this solid theoretical foundation.

NOTE

1. The symbolic meaning of an activity or product.

REFERENCES

Ap, J. (1992). *Understanding host resident perceptions of the impacts of tourism though social exchange theory.* Unpublished doctoral dissertation. Texas A&M University, College Station.

Backman, S. J. (1991). Exploring the relationship between perceived constraints and loyalty. *Journal of Leisure Research, 23,* 332-344.

Backman, S., & Crompton, J. (1990a). Differentiating between high, spurious, latent, and low loyalty participants in two leisure services. *Journal of Park and Recreation Administration, 9*(2), 1-17.

Backman, S., & Crompton, J. (1990b). The usefulness of selected variables for predicting activity loyalty. *Leisure Sciences, 13,* 205-220.

Bello, D. C., & Etzel, M. J. (1985). The role of novelty in the pleasure travel experience. *Journal of Travel Research, 23,* 20-26.

Berlyne, D. E. (1960). *Conflict, arousal, and curiosity.* New York: McGraw-Hill.

Bloch, P. H., Black, W. C., & Lichtenstein, D. (1989). Involvement with the equipment component of sport: Links to recreational commitment. *Leisure Sciences, 11,* 187-200.

Brown, G. P. (1991). Tourism and place-identity (Doctoral dissertation, Texas A&M University, 1990). *Dissertation Abstract International, 51,* 3516A.

Buchanan, T. (1985). Commitment and leisure behavior: A theoretical perspective. *Leisure Sciences, 7,* 401-420.

Celuch, K..G., & Longfellow, T. A. (1992). Consumers' service involvement: An exploratory examination. *Psychological Reports, 71,* 959-970.

Cohen, E. (1972). Towards a sociology of international research. *Social Research, 39,* 164-182.

Cohen, E. (1974). Who is a tourist? *Sociological Review, 22*(4), 527-533.

Cohen, E. (1979). A phenomenology of tourist experiences. *Sociology, 13,* 179-201.

Cosenza, R. M., & Davis, D. L. (1981). Family vacation decision making over the family life cycle: A decision and influence structure analysis. *Journal of Travel Research, 20*(2), 17-23.

Crompton, J. (1979). Motivations for pleasure vacation. *Journal of Leisure Research, 6*, 408-424.

Crotts, J. C. (1993). Personality correlates of the novelty seeking drive. *Journal of Hospitality & Leisure Marketing, 1*(3), 7-29.

Dann, G. M. (1981). Tourist motivation: An appraisal. *Annals of Tourism Research, 8*(2), 187-219.

Day, G. S. (1969). A two-dimensional concept of brand loyalty. *Journal of Advertising Research, 9*, 29-35.

Dimanche, F. (in press). Cross-cultural tourism marketing research: An assessment and recommendations for future studies. *Journal of International Consumer Marketing.*

Dimanche, F., Havitz, M. E., & Howard, D. R. (1991). Testing the Involvement Profile (IP) scale in the context of selected recreational and touristic activities. *Journal of Leisure Research, 23*(1), 51-66.

Dimanche, F., Havitz, M. E., & Howard, D. R. (1993). Consumer involvement profiles as a tourism segmentation tool. *Journal of Travel and Tourism Marketing, 1*(4), 33-52.

Dimanche, F., & Samdahl, D. (1991, October). *Leisure as symbolic consumption: A conceptualization and prospects for future research.* Paper presented at the NRPA Symposium on Leisure Research, Baltimore, MD.

Fesenmaier, D. R., & Johnson, B. (1989). Involvement-based segmentation: Implications for travel marketing in Texas. *Tourism Management, 10*(4), 293-300.

Filiatrault, P., & Ritchie, J. R. B. (1980). Joint purchasing decisions: A comparison of influence structure in family and couple decision making units. *Journal of Consumer Research, 7*, 131-140.

Havitz, M. E., & Dimanche, F. (1990). Propositions for testing the involvement construct in recreational and touristic contexts. *Leisure Sciences, 12*, 179-195.

Howard, D. R., & Havitz, M. E. (1993, October). *How enduring is enduring involvement?* Paper presented at the NRPA Symposium on Leisure research, San Jose, CA.

Howard, D. R., & Madrigal, R. (1990). Who makes the decision: The parent or the child? The perceived influence of parents and children on the purchase of recreation services. *Journal of Leisure Research, 22*, 244-258.

Hunt, J. (1961). *Intelligence and experience.* New York: The Ronald Press.

Jacoby, J., & Chestnut, R. W. (1978). *Brand loyalty measurement and management.* New York: Wiley.

Jarvis, L. P., & Mayo, E. J. (1986). Winning the market share game. *Cornell Hotel & Restaurant Administration Quarterly, 27*(3), 73-79.

Jenkins, R. I. (1978). Family decision-making. *Journal of Travel Research, 16*(4), 2-7.

Kahle, L. R., & Timmer, S. G. (1983). A theory and method for studying values. In L. R. Kahle (Ed.), *Social values and social change: Adaptation to life in America* (pp. 43-69). New York: Praeger.

Laurent, G., & Kapferer, J. N. (1985). Measuring consumer involvement profiles. *Journal of Marketing Research, 22* (February), 41-53.

Lee, T. H., & Crompton, J. (1992). Measuring novelty seeking in tourism. *Annals of Tourism Research, 19,* 732-751.

Madrigal, R. (1990). *An investigation of spouses' relative influence as it pertains to vacation decision making.* Unpublished doctoral dissertation. University of Oregon, Eugene.

Madrigal, R. (1993, October). *Personal values, personality, and tourist behavior.* Paper presented at the 1993 NRPA Symposium on Leisure Research, San Jose, CA.

Madrigal, R., Havitz, M. E., & Howard, D. R. (1992). Married couples' involvement with family vacations. *Leisure Sciences, 14,* 287-301.

Mansfeld, Y. (1992). From motivation to actual travel. *Annals of Tourism Research, 19,* 399-419.

McIntyre, N. (1989). The personal meaning of participation: Enduring involvement. *Journal of Leisure Research, 21*(2), 167-179.

McIntyre, N., & Pigram, J. J. (1992). Recreation specialization reexamined: The case of vehicle-based campers. *Leisure Sciences, 14,* 3-13.

McQuarrie, E. F., & Munson, J. M. (1987). The Zaichkowsky Personal Involvement Inventory: Modification and extension. *Advances in Consumer Research, 14,* 36-40.

Mo, C., Havitz D. R., & Howard, M. E. (1993, June). *Segmenting travel markets with the International Tourist Role (ITR) scale.* Paper presented at the 24th annual TTRA conference, Whistler, BC.

Mo, C., Howard, D. R., & Havitz, M. E. (1993). Testing an international tourist role typology. *Annals of Tourism Research, 20,* 319-335.

Moutinho, L. (1987). Consumer behavior in tourism. *European Journal of Marketing, 21*(10), 5-44.

Myers, P. B., & Moncrief, L. W. (1978). Differential leisure travel decision making between spouses. *Annals of Tourism Research, 5,* 157-165.

Neal, J. U. (1992). *Kids as customers: A handbook of marketing to children.* New York: Lexington Books.

Nichols, C. M., & Snepenger, D. J. (1988). Family decision making and tourism behavior and attitudes. *Journal of Travel Research, 26*(4), 2-6.

Norman, B. (1991). The influence of constraints on the generic decision of whether or not to take a summer vacation. In C. Sylvester & L. Caldwell (Eds.), *Abstracts from the 1991 Symposium on Leisure Research* (p. 59). Arlington, VA: National Recreation and Park Administration.

Orthner, D. K., & Mancini, J. A. (1990). Leisure impacts on family interaction and cohesion. *Journal of Leisure Research, 22,* 125-137.

Parasuraman, A., Zeithaml, V., & Berry, L. (1985). A conceptual model of service quality and its implications for future research. *Journal of Marketing, 49*(Fall), 41-50.

Parasuraman, A., Zeithaml, V., & Berry, L. (1988). SERVQUAL: A multiple-item scale for measuring consumer perceptions of service quality. *Journal of Retailing*, 64(Spring), 12-40.

Pearce, P. L. (1982). *The social psychology of tourist behavior.* New York: Pergamon.

Pearce, P. L. (1985). A systematic comparison of travel-related roles. *Human Relations*, 38(11), 1001-1011.

Plog, S. C. (1974). Why destination areas rise and fall in popularity. The *Cornell Hotel and Restaurant Administration Quarterly*, 14(4), 55-58.

Plog, S. C. (1990). A carpenter's tools: An answer to Stephen L. J. Smith's review of psychocentrism/allocentrism. *Journal of Travel Research*, 28(Spring), 43-45.

Plog, S. C. (1991). A carpenter's tools revisited: Measuring allocentrism and psychocentrism properly . . . the first time. *Journal of Travel Research*, 29(4), 51.

Plog, S. C. (1991). *Leisure travel: Making it a growth market . . . Again!* New York: Wiley

Pritchard, M. (1992). Development of the psychological commitment instrument for measuring travel service loyalty (Doctoral dissertation, University of Oregon, 1991). *Dissertation Abstracts International*, 52, 4408A

Pritchard, M., & Howard, D. R. (1993). Measuring loyalty in travel services: A multi-dimensional approach. *Proceedings of the World Marketing Congress, 6*, 115-119.

Pritchard, M., Howard, D. R., & Havitz, M. E. (1992). Loyalty measurement: A critical examination and theoretical extension. *Leisure Sciences, 14*, 155-164.

Reid, I. S., & Crompton, J. L. (1993). A taxonomy of leisure purchase decision paradigms based on level of involvement. *Journal of Leisure Research, 25*, 182-202.

Reinecke Flynn, L., & Goldsmith, R. E. (1993). Identifying innovators in consumer service markets. *The Service Industries Journal, 13*(3), 97-109.

Richins, M. L., Bloch, P. H., & McQuarrie, E. F. (1992). How enduring and situational involvement combine to create involvement responses. *Journal of Consumer Psychology, 1*(2), 143-153.

Rothschild, M. L. (1984). Perspectives on involvement: Current problems and future directions. *Advances in Consumer Research, 11*, 216-217.

Samdahl, D. M. (1988). A symbolic interactionist model of leisure: Theory and empirical support. *Leisure Sciences, 10*(1), 27-39.

Selin, S. W., & Howard, D. R. (1988). Ego involvement and leisure behavior: A conceptual specification. *Journal of Leisure Research, 20*(3), 237-244.

Shaw, S. M. (1992). Dereifying family leisure: An examination of women's and men's everyday experiences and perceptions of family time. *Leisure Sciences, 14*, 271-286.

Siegenthaler, K. L., & Lam, T. C. M. (1992). Commitment and ego-involvement in recreational tennis. *Leisure Sciences, 14*, 303-315.

Smith, S. L. (1990a). A test of Plog's allocentric/psychocentric model: Evidence from seven nations. *Journal of Travel Research, 28*(Spring), 40-43.

Smith, S. L. (1990b). Another look at the carpenter's tools: A reply to Plog. *Journal of Travel Research, 29*(Fall), 50-51.

Snepenger, D. J. (1987). Segmenting the vacation market by novelty-seeking role. *Journal of Travel Research, 26*(2), 8-14.

Solomon, M. R. (1992). *Consumer behavior.* Boston: Allyn & Bacon

Twynam, G. D. (1993). An analysis of the extent and response forms of complaint behavior and those factors which influence consumers to complain within travel contexts (Doctoral dissertation, University of Oregon, 1992). *Dissertation Abstracts International, 53,* 2983A.

Urry, J. (1990). The 'consumption' of tourism. *Sociology, 24*(1), 23-35.

Veldkamp, C. A., & Backman, S. J. (1992). Examination of the relationship between service quality and user loyalty. In L. Caldwell & C. Riddick (Eds), *Abstracts from the 1992 Symposium on Leisure Research* (p. 52). Arlington, VA: National Recreation and Park Association.

van Raaij, W. F. (1986). Consumer research on tourism: Mental and behavioral constructs. *Annals of Tourism Research, 13,* 1-9.

van Raaij, W. F., & Francken, D. A. (1984). Vacation decisions, activities and satisfactions. *Annals of Tourism Research, 11,* 101-112.

Watkins, M. (1987). The influence of involvement and information search on consumers' choice of recreation activities (Doctoral dissertation, University of Oregon, 1986). *Dissertation Abstract International, 47,* 3560A.

Yiannakis, A., & Gibson, H. (1992). Roles tourists play. *Annals of Tourism Research, 19,* 287-303.

Zaichkowsky, J. L. (1985). Measuring the involvement construct. *Journal of Consumer Research, 12*(December), 341-352.

Zeithaml, V. A., Parasuraman, A., & Berry, L. (1985). Problems and strategies in services marketing. *Journal of Marketing, 49,* 33-46.

The Influence of Friends and Relatives in Travel Decision-Making

Richard Gitelson
Deborah Kerstetter

SUMMARY. The objective of this exploratory study was to determine the extent to which friends and/or relatives influence the travel decision-making process beyond the role of information provider. The sample for this study was non-locals visiting three historic sites in Pennsylvania. Seventy-five percent of the groups sampled were visiting friends and/or relatives in the region. Respondents were requested to indicate (based on an allocation of 100%) who within the group had made various trip-related decisions. Friends and/or relatives were found to play a dominant role or were the sole decision maker between 29% and 39% of all decisions, respectively. The results indicated that friends and/or relatives shape behavior in a more direct fashion than previously documented.

INTRODUCTION

Travel marketers spend a great deal of time and money trying to influence tourists to visit their destination and, if successful, tourist's decisions about what to do and see in the area, where to eat, where to stay, etc. For

Richard Gitelson and Deborah Kerstetter are affiliated with the Recreation and Park Management Program at the School of Hotel, Restaurant & Recreation Management, 201 Mateer Building, The Pennsylvania State University, University Park, PA 16802.

Please send correspondence in care of Richard Gitelson, Recreation and Park Management Program, School of Hotel, Restaurant & Recreation Management, The Pennsylvania State University, 201 Mateer Building, University Park, PA 16802.

[Haworth co-indexing entry note]: "The Influence of Friends and Relatives in Travel Decision-Making." Gitelson, Richard, and Deborah Kerstetter. Co-published simultaneously in the *Journal of Travel & Tourism Marketing* (The Haworth Press, Inc.) Vol. 3, No. 3, 1994, pp. 59-68; and: *Economic Psychology of Travel and Tourism* (ed: John C. Crotts, and W. Fred van Raaij), The Haworth Press, Inc., 1994, pp. 59-68. Multiple copies of this article/chapter may be purchased from The Haworth Document Delivery Center [1-800-3-HAWORTH; 9:00 a.m. - 5:00 p.m. (EST)].

59

example, according to the U. S. Travel Data Center (1993), state tourism bureaus spent over $100 million in 1992-93 promoting their respective states as tourism destinations. In order to efficiently and effectively utilize advertising dollars state travel bureaus and others involved in the promotion of a tourist destination need to understand consumer behavior related to travel decisions, such as the planning frame(s) of tourists, their sources and use of information, and their overall decision making process(es).

Although there are numerous facets involved in the decision-making process, one area that has begun to receive more attention is the issue of who makes the decision within the travel group. This interest stems from a number of factors. First, a tourism experience appears to be a highly social event, i.e., involving two or more people in the travel group and the likelihood that many of these trips involves visiting family or friends. Second, destination and attraction marketers must design their advertising based on their knowledge of who will be using the information to make various types of decisions.

Most attempts to understand the dynamics of group decision-making related to travel decisions have focused on the role of the spouse/partner or the children in the process. Very few, if any, research efforts have focused on the role of friends and/or relatives in the decision making process, beyond the role this group plays in providing information to what are considered the primary decision makers. There would appear to be a number of reasons why this latter group should be considered as a more dynamic element of the decision process. First, if we are visiting an area for the first time, it would seem logical that we might defer at least some of the decision-making to individuals who are more knowledgeable about the destination area. Second, the friends/relatives may in a number of instances become part of the group visiting a particular attraction. The objective of this exploratory study then was to determine the extent to which friends and/or relatives influence the decision-making process beyond the role of information provider.

REVIEW OF THE LITERATURE

The available literature related to decision-making is quite extensive. Much of the early literature focused on individual decision-making but it has become readily apparent that the focus should be on the social group (Gupta, Hagerty & Myers, 1983). Most of the research in this area has focused on the family, specifically the husband/wife dyad and the parent/ child dyad (Darley & Lim, 1986; Howard & Madrigal, 1990; Moschis & Moore, 1984).

With respect to travel, studies have addressed various aspects of consumer behavior, including: the planning process (Gitelson & Crompton, 1983), information search (Fodness, 1992; van Raaij & Francken, 1984) and novelty seeking behavior (Snepenger, 1987). Additionally, studies have focused specifically on the involvement level of various members of the travel party in the decision-making process (Jenkins, 1979; Myers & Moncrief, 1978; Nichols & Snepenger, 1988; Ritchie & Filiatrault, 1980). The focus has usually been on the involvement levels of the husband/wife in various types of decisions related to travel, but there has been a growing recognition of the need to include other family members and friends and/or relatives.

Although patterns of consumer behavior are likely to be learned during pre-adult years and persist well into adulthood, Moschis (1987) suggests that as individuals encounter new situations the salience of reference groups, including friends and relatives, is likely to change. Bellenger and Moschis (1981) found that peers play a significant role in the formation of consumer patronage behavior. More specifically, Becherer and Morgan (1982), replicating a study by Moschis (1976), found that an individual's propensity to seek and rely upon information from a reference group is related to the degree of perceived similarity with these groups.

Crompton (1981), in his research on pleasure travel, has suggested that friends and/or relatives influence behavior throughout the recreation experience. From the perspective of providing information to decision-makers, the influence of friends and/or relatives has been well documented (Bultena & Field, 1980; Jenkins, 1978; van Raaij & Francken, 1984; West, 1982). In fact, when asked what sources provide trip-related information, friends and/or relatives are usually listed as the most frequent and most credible source (Capella & Greco, 1987; Gitelson & Crompton, 1983).

Reference groups, including friends and relatives, are also important factors in the overall decision-making process. According to Peter and Olson (1994), reference groups exert a major influence over most aspects of consumer behavior, especially the decision-making process. They influence decision makers in three ways. The first type of influence involves the provision of information, which is used or not used by the decision-maker based on the perception that the information is useful and the reference group member is credible. The second type of influence is utilitarian in nature. This occurs when a member of a reference group provides a reward or sanction for something that the decision maker has done. The third type of influence is exerted on the decision maker's self concept and is called value-expressive influence.

In this paper friends and/or relatives are treated as part of the decision-making group, not as part of a reference group. Thus, the friend and/or relative is considered an equal to other members of the group with whom they visit a particular site. The emphasis of this analysis was to determine the extent to which various members of the travel group (including all members, not just household members) made selected travel-related decisions.

METHODOLOGY

The respondents in this study were visiting three sites in Southwestern Pennsylvania; the Johnstown Flood Memorial, the Allegheny Portage National Historic Site, and/or the Horseshoe Curve. The overall objective of the study was to evaluate efforts that were being made by the America's Industrial Heritage Project (AIHP) to promote the first leg of a Heritage Route which now includes 13 sites. The current Heritage Route is 43 miles long, with plans to add another 500 miles in the next 2 years. Part of the study was to develop a profile of Route users and to begin looking at their decision-making process.

Interviews were conducted over a five-week period during the summer of 1992. Individuals were asked to respond to a one-page questionnaire. Upon completion they were asked for their address and given a follow-up questionnaire which was to be completed when they returned home. The refusal rate on-site was less than two percent. Three additional contacts were made to non-respondents and the final response rate for the follow-up portion of the study was seventy-eight percent. Although this sample was not large, a companion study at the site, which randomly sampled 425 additional individuals from June through October, indicated that the smaller sample was representative of visitors to these sites.

The study differentiated between locals (individuals who lived within a nine-county area containing the America's Industrial Heritage Project) or non-locals (all others). For the purpose of this study, analysis was limited to non-locals who visited the site with friends and/or relatives and/or who were visiting friends and/or relatives in the region (n = 71). Four of the respondents did not complete the decision-making section of the survey and were eliminated from the analyses.

Respondents were requested to indicate (based on an allocation of 100%) who in the traveling party had made various trip-related decisions. These decisions included: (a) which sites to visit, (b) what to do in the area, (c) how long to stay in the area, (d) where to eat, (e) who was responsible for getting trip-related information, and (f) where to stay if the trip lasted for more than a day. Requesting individuals to allocate percentages has been proposed as a more effective way to determine decision making responsibilities than the use of three or five-point scales (Jenkins, 1978).

Based on the percentage allocation, each potential decision-maker was assigned a category. These categories included: (1) sole decision-maker, i.e., 100% responsible for the decision, (2) dominant influence, i.e., the greatest percentage allocation of any decision-maker, (3) shared influence, i.e., equal influence with at least one other decision-maker and more than any other decision-maker, (4) lesser role, i.e., a percentage of influence less than some other decision-maker, or (5) no influence.

For example, a respondent may have indicated that her group consisted of herself, a spouse, children and friends. If 100% was allocated to the spouse category for the decision "which sites to visit," then the spouse was considered the sole or "total" decision-maker. If, however, the percentage was evenly distributed between the respondent, the spouse, and the friend, then this was considered an "equally shared" decision. If 80% of the influence over the decision was allocated to the spouse, and 20% to the friend, then the spouse was considered "dominant," the friend was considered to have a lessor role, and the children and the respondent were considered to have played no role in that decision. Some of the types of decisions did not apply to all groups. For example, 24 of the groups did not spend the night in the region which meant the decision "where to stay" was not part of the decision-making process.

RESULTS

Individuals were asked to describe the group that was visiting the site in terms of whether or not a spouse, children, friends and/or relatives were included. Only three percent of the visitation from outside the region to the two AIHP sites was by a single individual (see Table 1). Over 70% of the groups contained a spouse or partner and 75% of the groups contained friends and/or relatives. Approximately one-fifth of the groups contained children.

Visiting friends and/or relatives was the most important factor in the respondents' decision to visit the region. Nearly 30% visited the region to view the scenery and 16% indicated other attractions besides the historic site were an important factor in their decision to visit the region.

The results indicated that the planning frame for this trip to the region was relatively short. Nearly 40% began planning for the trip on the day of the visit and only 14% began planning more than a month before the trip began. The duration of the trip was also rather short. Nearly six out of ten groups stayed in the region for only one day, and only seven percent

TABLE 1. Profile of groups included in the sample.

Composition of group visiting site (N = 71)		Reasons for visiting region (N = 68)	
Group consisted of:	Percentage		Percentage
Visited alone	3%	Visit friends/relatives	66%
Spouse/partner	72	View the scenery	29
Child(ren)	23	Visit another attraction	16
Friends/relatives	75	Personal business	13
		Attend special event	9
		To go shopping	6
		Business (nonpersonal)	0
		Attend a convention	0

When planning for trip to region began (N = 71)		Number of days stayed in region (N = 69)	
When planning began:	Percentage	Number of days	Percentage
Day of the visit	39%	1	59%
The week before	23	2	37
2 to 4 weeks before	24	3 days or more	7
1 to 3 months before	11		
4 or more months before	3	Had someone in group visited region (N = 64) before this visit	
			Percentage
		Yes	74%
		No	26

stayed more than two days. Nearly three-fourths (74%) of the groups had at least one member who had previously visited the region.

Results in Table 2 indicate that all of the travel-related decisions were influenced by friends and/or relatives. The extent to which friends and/or relatives played either the dominant or sole decision-making role ranged from 29% in the case of deciding how long the non-locals would stay to 39% in the decision process to decide what the non-locals would do while in the region. An additional 11% to 25% of the 6 decision areas were equally decided by friends and/or relatives and one or more other group members.

In slightly more than half of the decisions (54%), friends and/or relatives were not the dominant or sole decision-maker. Of the six decisions included in the study, friends and/or relatives were involved in at least one decision as the sole or dominant decision-maker in forty-seven percent of the cases. In approximately one-third of the groups (34%), friends and/or relatives dominated the decision-making process in at least four of the six types of decisions.

TABLE 2. Role played by friends and/or relatives in selected travel decisions.[a][b]

Level of Influence	Which sites (n = 67)	Length of stay (n = 66)	What to do (n = 67)	Where to eat (n = 64)	Trip info (n = 60)	Where to stay (n = 45)
Sole decision maker	25%	18%	21%	25%	27%	24%
Dominant role	13	11	18	11	10	9
Equal role	12	20	16	25	12	11
Lesser role	6	5	5	3	2	2
No role	43	47	40	36	50	54

Number of decisions where friends and/or relatives played total or dominant role

	Percentage
Did not play sole or dominant role in any decisions	54%
Sole or dominant decision maker in at least one type of decision	5
Sole or dominant decision maker in two or three decisions	8
Sole or dominant decision maker in four or more decisions	34

[a]Four surveys did not contain information on decision making and were excluded from the analyses.
[b]Not all types of decisions were applicable for each group. For example, the non locals in 22 groups did not stay overnight. Thus, the decision as to where to stay was not applicable for that group.

CONCLUSION

The fact that nearly 75% of non-locals, as defined in this study as living outside a nine-county region, were visiting friends and/or relatives that lived within the region is noteworthy, but more striking is the degree of influence these individuals have in the decision-making process. Past studies have limited their focus to the role these friends and/or relatives play in providing decision-makers with information. But these results indicated that friends and/or relatives shape behavior in a more direct fashion, and, in many cases, take on the role of "sole" decision-maker. Thus, future research efforts need to include friends and/or relatives as potentially equal partners in the decision-making process, just as they have done with the spouse/partner and children.

Although this study was exploratory and further research is needed, the findings suggest the importance of marketing to locals. It appears that in many cases, visitors to the region are deferring major decisions to individuals more likely to be familiar with what the local area has to offer. In the present case study, the Route marketers are now reviewing their advertising mix, which before this study had been heavily skewed to target markets outside the nine-county region. The study results may not be as important to destinations with large, well-known attractions like Orlando, but certainly appear warranted in areas with lesser known attractions such as this nine-county area.

A number of important issues related to the decision-making process deserve attention in future research efforts. At what point in time do friends and/or relatives become influential? For example, do friends and/or relatives impact the decision-making process prior to, during, and/or after the trip has begun? Andereck (1992) suggests that information related to the timing of various decisions would allow researchers to better understand tourist behavior and, as a result of this knowledge, help tourism marketers and suppliers to more effectively target their market(s).

This study examined six primary or "functional" decisions common to pleasure travel. It did not include "non-functional" types of decisions which may be integral components of pleasure travel decision-making. Fesenmaier, Vogt and McKay (1992) have found that individuals may seek input, perhaps from friends and/or relatives, on books or films, for example, which can evoke memories about their visit or allow them to experience the destination without actually visiting it. Or, individuals may seek advice, perhaps again from friends and/or relatives, with respect to educational materials about the destination in order to enhance their knowledge of the area. Future research efforts may want to incorporate "non-functional" types of decisions into their study designs when studying the influence of friends and/or relatives in the decision-making process.

Finally, there were a number of inherent limitations in this study which can be addressed in future studies. The sample was rather small and was taken at three historic sites in southwestern Pennsylvania. Thus, it would be beneficial to extend this research to other types of attractions. Also, with larger sample sizes, more sophisticated analyses can be used to determine the relative roles of various group members. Only one individual was asked to indicate his or her perception of who took part in making various types of decisions. Future studies would benefit from having more than one perspective as to what role various group members played.

REFERENCES

Andereck, K. (1992). Comments on researching consumer information. *Proceedings of the 23rd Annual Conference of the Travel and Tourism Research Association* (pp. 50-52). Minneapolis, Minnesota: Travel and Tourism Research Association.

Becherer, R., & Morgan, F. (1982). Informal group/influence among situationally/ dispositionally oriented consumers. *Journal of the Academy of Marketing Science*, 10(Summer): 269-281.

Bellenger, D., & Moschis, G. (1981). A socialization model of retail patronage. In K. Monroe (Ed.), *Advances in consumer research* (pp. 373-378). Ann Arbor, Michigan: Association for Consumer Research.

Bultena, G. L., & Field, D. R. (1980). Structural effects in national park going. *Leisure Sciences*, 3(3): 221-240.

Capella, L., & Greco, A. (1987). Information sources of elderly for vacation decisions. *Annals of Tourism Research*, 14(1): 148-151.

Clawson, M., & Knetsch, J. (1966). *Economics of Outdoor Recreation*. Baltimore: John Hopkins.

Crompton, J. (1981). Dimensions of the social group role in pleasure vacations. *Annals of Tourism Research*, 8(4): 550-567.

Darley, W., & Lim, J. (1986). Family decision making in leisure-time activities: An exploratory investigation of the impact of locus of control, child age influence factor and parental type on perceived child influence. In R. J. Lutz (Ed.), *Advances in Consumer Research* (pp. 370-374). Ann Arbor: Association for Consumer Research.

Fesenmaier, D., Vogt, C., & MacKay, K. (1992). Exploring the role of pre-trip information search in travel decisions. *Proceedings of the 23rd Annual Conference of the Travel and Tourism Research Association* (pp. 32-36). Minneapolis, Minnesota: Travel and Tourism Research Association.

Fodness, D. (1992). The impact of family life cycle on the vacation decision-making process. *Journal of Travel Research*, 31(2): 8-13.

Gitelson, R., & Crompton, J. (1983). The planning horizons and sources of information used by pleasure vacationers. *Journal of Travel Research*, 21(3): 2-7.

Gupta, S., Hagerty, M., & Myers, J. (1983). New directions in family decision making research. In R. Bagozzi & A. Tybout (Eds.), *Advances in Consumer Research* (pp. 445-449). Ann Arbor: Association for Consumer Research.

Howard, D., & Madrigal, R. (1990). Who makes the decision: The parent or the child? The perceived influence of parents and children on the purchase of recreation services. *Journal of Leisure Research*, 22(3): 244-258.

Jenkins, R. (1978). The influence of children in family decision-making: Parents perceptions. *Advances in Consumer Research*, 6: 413-418.

Jenkins, R. (1979). Family vacation decision-making. *Journal of Travel Research*, 16(4): 2-7.

Moschis, G. (1976). Social comparison and informal group influence. *Journal of Marketing Research*, 13 (August): 237-244.

Moschis, G. (1987). *Consumer socialization: A life-cycle perspective.* Lexington, Massachusetts: Lexington Books.

Moschis, G., & Moore, R. (1984). Anticipatory consumer socialization. *Journal of the Academy of Marketing Science,* 12(4): 109-123.

Myers, P., & Moncrief, L. (1978). Differential leisure travel decision making between spouses. *Annals of Tourism Research,* 5: 157-165.

Nichols, C., & Snepenger, D. (1988). Family decision making and tourism behavior and attitudes. *Journal of Travel Research,* 26(4): 2-6.

Peter, J. P., & Olson, J. C. (1994). *Understanding consumer behavior.* Boston, Massachusetts: Irwin.

Ritchie, J. R., & Filiatrault, P. (1980). Family vacation decision-making. *Journal of Travel Research,* 18(4): 3-14.

Snepenger, D. J. (1987). Segmenting the vacation market by novelty-seeking role. *Journal of Travel Research,* 26(2): 8-14.

U. S. Travel Data Center (1993). *Survey of state travel offices: 1992-93.* Washington, DC: U. S. Travel Data Center.

van Raaij, F., & Francken, D. (1984). Vacation decisions, activities, and satisfactions. *Annals of Tourism Research,* 11(1): 101-112.

West, P. C. (1982). A nationwide test of the status group dynamics approach to outdoor recreation demand. *Leisure Sciences,* 5(1): 1-18.

Toward a Dynamic Model of Complex Tourism Choices: The Seasonal Home Location Decision

Susan I. Stewart
Daniel J. Stynes

SUMMARY. Both economics and psychology are rich with theories and methods relating to the purchasing behavior of the consumer. Studies of tourism decision making mirror more general applications of choice and decision modeling, focusing on discrete choices made from a known and fixed set of alternatives. This approach works best for highly structured, routine decision situations. Many common assumptions employed in decision modeling are violated in more complex, long-range choices, which are common in tourism. Based on a review of decision making research and a study of the seasonal home location decision using verbal protocol methods, a dynamic model of complex choice is proposed.

INTRODUCTION

Decision research is one of the major areas where economics and psychology meet (Hammond, McClelland & Mumpower, 1980). Each

---

Susan Stewart is a doctoral candidate at Michigan State University and Research Social Scientist at the North Central Forest Experiment Station in Chicago, IL. Daniel Stynes is Professor in the Department of Park and Recreation Resources at Michigan State University, East Lansing, MI.
The research reported in this article was supported by the USDA Forest Service, North Central Forest Experiment Station.

[Haworth co-indexing entry note]: "Toward a Dynamic Model of Complex Tourism Choices: The Seasonal Home Location Decision." Stewart, Susan I., and Daniel J. Stynes. Co-published simultaneously in the *Journal of Travel & Tourism Marketing* (The Haworth Press, Inc.) Vol. 3, No. 3, 1994, pp. 69-88; and: *Economic Psychology of Travel and Tourism* (ed: John C. Crotts, and W. Fred van Raaij), The Haworth Press, Inc., 1994, pp. 69-88. Multiple copies of this article/chapter may be purchased from The Haworth Document Delivery Center [1-800-3-HAWORTH; 9:00 a.m. - 5:00 p.m. (EST)].

69

discipline is rich with theories and methods relating to the decision making behavior of the consumer. Many of these have been applied in tourism settings, including Anderson and Louviere's conjoint choice model (Goodrich, 1978; Haider & Ewing, 1990), Fishbein's expectancy-value model (Um & Crompton, 1990), and Ericsson and Simon's process tracing methods (Vining & Fishwick, 1991).

For the most part, tourism applications mirror more general applications of choice and decision modeling, focusing principally on discrete choices made from a known and fixed set of alternatives. This approach works best for highly structured, routine decision situations. However, many common assumptions employed in decision modeling are violated when choices are complex and involve longer time periods, both for decision making and for consumption of the chosen alternative.

Complex choices are fundamentally different from simple, routine purchases (Arndt, 1976). Economist Karen Gredal (1966) coined the term *strategic goods* for major purchases with long term implications. As Arndt describes the concept, "Certain buying decisions are strategic in that they are concerned with the long term binding up of financial resources . . . They affect the budget available for other goods and services" (Arndt, 1976, p. 214). This description fits many of the purchases made in connection with recreation and tourism. For example, when one purchases a boat, recreational vehicle, or off-road vehicle, the initial cost is considerable, and is followed by additional expenses associated with operation, maintenance, and storage. Buying a seasonal home or a time share in a condominium also requires a long term commitment of resources, and in addition, will shape future vacation decisions. The long term commitment of resources and consumption over time involves risk and uncertainty, which makes the task of judging alternatives difficult for the decision maker (Abelson & Levi, 1985). Complex decisions may also take the decision maker a long time to resolve, and the passage of time can compound the complications when circumstances affecting the decision change with time. These dynamics cast further doubt on the wisdom of applying traditional static or atemporal choice models to complex choice processes.

This paper will explore development of a model of decision making associated with long term, complex purchase processes. The lengthy decision process associated with complex purchases creates more opportunities than usual for marketers to assist, direct and influence a buyer's choice, but to do so they must understand both how and when in an extended choice process potential buyers are most easily reached. As part of a larger study of seasonal home buying, this paper will examine the nature of the seasonal home location decision process, using verbal protocol interviews with seasonal home buyers. Following a review of decision making literature, the protocol results are presented and analyzed. The paper concludes with a proposed model of a complex decision process.

DECISION LITERATURE

The process of choosing one alternative over others involves making a series of decisions in which an individual's motivations, preferences, knowledge, cognitive processes, resources, and constraints all play a role. Research into the behaviors and consequences of decision making is conducted in many fields, each with a slightly different theoretical and methodological emphasis. Abelson and Levi (1985), in an extensive review of decision research, propose classifying decision making studies as either *structural* or *process* oriented. They state that:

Structural models are concerned with describing the relationship between stimulus and response or between input and output. *Process models*, in contrast, focus on the transformation process that occurs between the stimulus and response. (Abelson & Levi, 1985; p. 235, italics theirs)

Structural models are frequently grounded in economic theories of consumer choice, while process models rely more heavily on psychological theories of perception, learning, and judgement. The research objectives and methods used to test the two classes of models reflect these different origins.

Structural Models

Most applications of decision research to recreation and tourism utilize discrete choice models, in particular multinomial logit models (Stynes & Peterson, 1984) used together with conjoint scaling methods (Louviere, 1983; Louviere & Timmermans, 1990a). Conjoint choice models predict a consumer's choice based on (1) attributes of the alternatives in the choice set, (2) assumptions about how perceptions of the attributes are combined to form overall evaluations, and (3) the assumption that the individual will choose the alternative which maximizes her or his utility (Louviere, 1988). In recreation and tourism contexts, these models have been applied to studies of park visitation (Louviere & Timmermans, 1990b), the effect of park management options on park choice (Lieber & Fesenmair, 1984), and vacation destination choice (Goodrich, 1978; Haider & Ewing, 1990). Some researchers (e.g., Hammond et al., 1980) question how realistic structural models are in light of a wealth of literature suggesting that individuals are satisficers rather than optimizers (Simon, 1955), employ a wide variety of decision making heuristics or short cuts (Tversky & Kahneman, 1974), and more generally are not entirely "rational," in the sense of behaving as a normative decision making model would suggest they should (Abelson & Levi, 1985; Nisbett & Ross, 1980). Structural models are not considered useful as replica models of cognitive or behavioral processes (Hogarth, 1986), but rather as predictive tools.

Process Models

In contrast to predictive structural models, process models focus on how a choice is made, and argue that this process has much to do with which choice is made. Behavioral decision theory states that decision making involves learning and adaptation to the decision environment (Edwards, 1961; Einhorn & Hogarth, 1981). Learning can alter the decision maker's perception and judgement, and is most likely to occur when the decision maker is initially unfamiliar with the choice alternatives or the decision environment. Adaptation will be most important when the decision environment is unfamiliar, or when the environment changes over time (1985). Both of these conditions, an unfamiliar task and a changing decision environment, are most likely to be associated with complex choice, implying that learning and adaptation will be most important when choice is most complex.

Preferences and choice rules are considered outcomes of the learning and adaptation that occurs during the decision process, rather than fixed features of a decision maker or a type of decision task. The "heuristics and biases" identified by researchers such as Kahneman and Tversky (1979) are seen as adaptive mechanisms, rather than errors.

Other decision theories also support the concept of learning and adaptation during decision making. According to Newell and Simon (1972; Newell, Shaw, & Simon, 1958), each person needs to understand and interpret or frame the choice in their own terms before they begin trying to resolve it. In their model of problem solving, framing is proposed as a first step in solving a problem or making a choice. The frame coordinates and directs other decision making activities. Its idiosyncratic nature, together with its influence on decision making behavior, offers an explanation for why decision making varies across individuals (Haines, 1974). Information processing research focuses on the ways people deal with large amounts of information, and has shown how people create and use a variety of methods for searching and processing information to avoid being burdened with too much information, an example of adaptative decision making.

While structural models treat decision making as a static or atemporal event, dynamics are an implicit element of most process models, as the notion of a process implies some sequence of events. The concept of adaptive behavior, for example, assumes the decision maker will react to perceptual and environmental changes, and their decision making behavior will reflect that reaction.

Decision theory has moved from its origins in microeconomic consumer theory to a more psychologically based, empirically supported perspective which adds recognition of the importance of both environmental constraints and human cognitive limitations. The basis for decision making behavior in process theory encompasses both the economic concept of subjective expected utility maximization, and the psychological concepts of stimulus-response behavior and cognitive processing.

THE SEASONAL HOME LOCATION DECISION PROCESS

The purchase of a seasonal home is an example of a major, complex, leisure-related decision. For most households, the purchase of a seasonal home is second in price only to the purchase of a primary home, and may be owned, paid for, and used for as long, or longer. Durable goods are defined by the Department of Commerce as those which last for at least three years; seasonal homes are typically owned and used for a much longer period, making them a sort of "super durable," or strategic good. It is rare to purchase more than one seasonal home in a lifetime, and as a result, few individuals ever become experienced seasonal home buyers.

While permanent home location is constrained by place of work and family ties, the number of available seasonal home locations (i.e., the universal choice set) is practically infinite. The decision maker is likely to know about only a small subset of that universal choice set at the beginning of the decision process. Due to the absence of time pressure, the complexity of potential choice sets, and a lack of experience, most decision makers can be expected to take much longer to purchase a seasonal home than they would to purchase other major goods. During this time, the decision maker and the decision environment will change, making it difficult to predict when a choice will be made, or what form the decision task will take.

THE STUDY OF SEASONAL HOME BUYING

The unique nature of the seasonal home purchase makes the use of traditional decision process research techniques difficult. Because the seasonal home decision process occurs over an extended period of time, recording protocols concurrently, as is usually done in decision process research, was not practical. To record protocols concurrently, the process would need to be simulated in the laboratory. Creating a laboratory simulation of the decision process, however, precludes observation of the decision maker's response to the unique features of a long term, complex choice. For example, in a real world setting, the seasonal home buyer must construct and search a choice set from an almost infinite number of alternatives spread across hundreds of miles, a process difficult to mimic in the laboratory. The effects of change over time would also be difficult to recreate in a meaningful way in the laboratory.

In order to allow the process to unfold more naturally, we decided to use a combination of methods to study the decision process in the field. The first phase of the study involves the use of retrospective verbal protocol techniques to interview a small sample of seasonal home buyers. Based on these interviews, the model of complex choice was developed. These portions of the study are described here. Later stages of the study involve using a two-period, two-panel survey of currently active seasonal home buyers to test aspects of the proposed model.

The verbal protocol method is a qualitative data collection technique often used in process tracing studies of decision making. A verbal protocol is a record of a decision maker's thoughts, judgements, and decisions during a decision making process (Ericsson & Simon, 1984). Protocols can be recorded concurrently with the decision making process by asking the respondent to verbalize his or her thoughts while making a decision, or retrospectively, after the decision process has been completed (Ericsson & Simon, 1984). Verbal protocol interviewing is similar to other unstructured interview techniques, except that protocols focus on the events associated with one decision making process.

Verbal protocols are most often collected concurrently, with the decision taking place in a laboratory setting (Ford, Schmitt, Schechtman, Hults, & Doherty, 1989). Using verbal protocol methods retrospectively to facilitate field study raises questions about the decision maker's ability to recall the details of her or his decision (Ericsson & Simon, 1984). Psychological research suggests, however, that the recall of autobiographical events is affected by the nature of the event, and will be enhanced when an event has a major financial impact (Silberstein, 1989), is non-routine, and occurs over an extended period of time (Auriat, 1993; Bradburn, Rips &

Shevell, 1987; Rubin, 1986). While routine consumer purchases may be difficult to recall, the purchase of a seasonal home or any other strategic good is much more likely to be remembered.

Allowing the seasonal home decision to occur in the field rather than the laboratory is also expected to enhance recall. In laboratory decision making studies, subjects are not involved in initiating the decision process, defining the choice set, or deciding which attributes to attend to; these decisions are made by the researcher. While the laboratory subject engages in few memorable behaviors instrumental to the decision process, the decision maker in a field setting may travel to seasonal home areas, talk with real estate agents, talk with friends and family members, and so on. These actions reinforce memory of the event by providing additional cues to events and their sequence. In addition, telling others about the search process, sharing evaluations of alternatives, and discussing plans for further decision activities is a form of event rehearsal, which has been shown to enhance recall of events (Robinson, 1976).

METHODS

The population for this study includes people who are considering or have recently completed a seasonal home purchase. The sampling frame was generated using a snowball sampling technique, where each person interviewed is asked to suggest other people who might be interviewed. An effort was made to interview the actual decision making unit, whether an individual, couple, family, or other group. When this was not possible, the subject was encouraged to discuss the role of other group members in the decision process. In choosing subjects for the study, an effort was made to include decision makers who had started their decision process at different times, were currently engaged in different types of decision related activities, and were looking for seasonal homes in different geographic areas.

Interviews were conducted at a time and place of the subject's choosing. The length of the interviews varied depending on the subject, ranging from 15 minutes to more than an hour. Interviews began with a brief explanation of the research project, including its purpose and sponsors. In order to avoid biasing the subjects or influencing the way in which they present their account of the decision process, the description of the study's purpose was brief and general. Each subject gave us permission to tape the session.

Decision makers were asked to talk about the process they had gone through or were going through to find a seasonal home. They were asked to include all parts of the process, starting with the time they first considered buying a seasonal home to the present time, and to indicate the sequence in which things happened. Examples of the type and range of information sought from them were given when clarification was requested. Following this introduction, the interviewer interrupted as little as possible, and only for the purpose of encouraging continuation of the narrative, or redirecting the discussion to the topic of the decision process. Depending on how forthcoming the subject was, follow-up questions were sometimes asked. Each interview ended when the subject indicated that the whole story had been told.

RESULTS

Nine verbal protocols were collected during 1992-1993. The grounded theory method of open coding was used in protocol analysis (Strauss & Corbin, 1990). This technique of analyzing interview data emphasizes development of categories and identification of important variables as outcomes of, rather than inputs to, analysis. Unlike most verbal protocol studies which attempt to identify specific choice rules and search procedures (Ford et al., 1989) our analysis emphasized investigation of the temporal, spatial, and dynamic aspects of seasonal home decision making.

The sample includes five decision makers who had recently purchased seasonal homes, one who had recently considered a purchase but decided against it, one who was still considering a purchase but decided to delay further action, and two decision makers who had just begun to actively consider a purchase. Of those we interviewed, all but one were making their purchase decision with one or more other people. In two cases, we were able to interview a couple.

All but two decision makers were considering or had purchased homes in northwest lower Michigan, although some of these people had also considered sites in central Michigan and in northeast lower Michigan. The remainder were interested in southwest Michigan, on the Lake Michigan coast. Other regions of the country had also been considered by some buyers.

Decision makers differed in preferences for neighborhood settings, natural settings, recreation resources, and community types. Of those who had purchased a seasonal home, most reported having spent about 10 years considering a purchase, and 3-5 years actively searching (working with a realtor, driving around potential areas).

While the decision process was somewhat different for each decision maker, three general stages or sets of events emerged which were common to all but one decision maker interviewed. The earliest activities associated with the seasonal home decision process involved forming a decision frame. The following excerpt is from an interview with a man who has just begun to look for a seasonal home. He is tentative about many elements of his decision frame, recognizing the possibility of changes in the decision environment that might affect his decision:

> ... we began staying at a place near Pentwater and on the beach on Lake Michigan. My wife had never been, never stayed on a cottage on the lake before and she just fell in love with being there . . . I think it is the most beautiful beach in Michigan. And so we kind of decided that we were going to start saving and looking for ways to find a place on Lake Michigan. We talked to two of our friends and there is a possibility . . . that this would be either a two family or a three family place. We thought about the tax benefits too. . . . I would think that the second home tax deduction would perhaps go away in the coming four years . . . . But that wouldn't be a deterrent to us at all. So, . . . we started putting oh a few hundred dollars a month into a different mutual fund just to save, to get together a down payment. We decided to start calling, have not placed any calls yet. Start calling real estate firms in the cities that are proximate to the lake, all the way from Muskegon up to the northern part of the Lower Peninsula. We would rather be south, because of the proximity to Lansing and reduction of travel time, but we would go north if pricing made a difference. I don't know if it does or not.

At this point, he has a general idea about the location he prefers, the financial requirements and how he will meet them, and a strategy for beginning to actively search. The statement he ends with is typical of the first stage; he has considered sacrificing proximity to home for a lower price, but does not know whether it is necessary to make that trade-off. While uncertainty was common in the first stages, decision makers differed in what they were uncertain about; for some, motives were difficult to sort out, while for others, gauging marginal costs of attributes was a greater concern.

First stage activities also served to create a more manageable decision task. Eliminating parts of the choice and criteria sets offers the decision maker a way to simplify the search process, and to make it more efficient by focusing in on just the alternatives that are most likely to be satisfactory, as this decision maker describes doing:

> But what we did, we identified, rather than saying geez, this is really pretty, we sort of thought, well this is what we want and what we

> want we did it two ways. We decided what we didn't want. I don't want lakefront, I mean I would not be opposed to lakefront, but I'm not an aquatic kind of a guy, . . . and so we narrowed. We eliminated. Some people I know they got to be on the lake, either the big lake or the big bay . . . or else an inland lake. And that isn't a requirement for us. What sort of has been the requirement though is the golf course.

This excerpt provides a clear example of the elimination-by-aspects (EBA) choice rule, first proposed by Tversky (1972). In EBA, one attribute, in this case waterfront, is used to divide the choice set into acceptable and non-acceptable subsets. This is a non-compensatory choice rule, in that no value on other attributes or aspects (e.g., view) can compensate for its value on the chosen attribute, location on the waterfront. Non-compensatory choice rules appeared often in the early stages of decision making.

While previous process tracing research has treated all search activity as a tool for evaluation and choice decisions, these protocols indicate that search is also important in helping decision makers frame the decision. In the next interview, the decision maker discusses the transition between early search activities and later, more directed search efforts:

> Five years ago we didn't invest our time and take up somebody else's time and energy and thought process to help us out. We looked, you know, drive by stuff. And not just stuff, but drive by areas. And you know, I mean we've scoured, we semi-scoured northern Michigan and we've taken weekends that we just sort of gone up and maybe we'll stay with my family in West Branch and then we will just head, you know, north and a little bit east, or a little bit west and take Lake Huron or take ah, Lake Michigan or Grand Traverse, or Little Traverse Bay and just sort of look around and talk to friends . . . so we thought well let's, couple years ago and we thought well let's start to ah, talk to people, [to real estate agents], you know.

At this point, the decision maker feels he has resolved enough of the uncertainty about the seasonal home market, and about his preferences, to feel comfortable contacting a real estate agent. One unusual feature of this person's search activities is the absence of nesting, or first choosing an area, then considering specific properties (McFadden, 1978). Most decision makers nested their search early in the process, before contacting an agent. The prevalence of nesting in seasonal home search may be due to the geographical limits on any one real estate agent's territory, although it also serves to limit the decision maker's travel costs. This person dealt with the agents' limitations by working with several; the other decision makers who did not use a nesting strategy worked without an agent, and reported visiting areas " . . . anywhere from two hours away from us to four to five hours away from us." They describe their search strategy:

> We would just go to the local little store and we'd say, do you know of any places for sale. Well some of them aren't in the real estate magazines, don't go to realtors. They just put them up for sale by word of mouth. So that, you know, we found quite a few different places that way.

During search, decision makers often reported changes in what they were looking for and how they went about finding it. Many changes arose as decision makers learned more about the relative costs of the features they wanted. This couple describes their experience trying to find a nice cottage in their price range in the Grand Traverse Bay area of Michigan:

> . . . every cottage we went to, you know, it was the price range we were looking at, we were not going to get a Taj Mahal and so . . . it was always something wrong, you know. We walked out on one that the dock was tilted like this. We were holding the kids up going, yeah, this would be fun.
> You make it sound like we're looking for a $20,000 cottage.
> No, you know what the prices are up there, I mean, you know, these were $100,000 places.

This couple eventually discovered that prices vary considerably with distance from Traverse City, and by re-orienting their search were able to find a seasonal home that met their expectations:

> . . . and I said, this is what I envision being able to buy and here it was. But we were surprised how . . . the price of property when you get above like Suttons Bay, drops.

For some decision makers, the budget, evaluation criteria, and search strategy developed early in the decision process did not change during the decision process. One couple who had recently purchased land where they are now building a seasonal home reported a very stable decision frame over the course of the 10 years they spent looking. Their criteria set was small; they wanted wooded property on an inland lake within their budget.

> Okay, we found our property in the newspaper. We've been looking for property about 10 to 12 years . . . we'd go up weekends and drive

around or camp and look for property and finally decided that we really wanted to stay in Michigan and we really wanted to stay on the west coast of Michigan. Because we liked it over there better than the east coast. And the [Upper Peninsula] was just too far for us to make it accessible to us during the week or during the regular working year . . . and ah one day in the newspaper there was an ad in the paper. And Bob said this sounds really good. Well we had been on some really wild goose-chases and I mean we were looking for property on a lake and we'd go and check things out and it would be a cow pond in a field, you know. And we were really getting frustrated, so when he said this sounds really good, I said right. So, okay, we decided to go up and take a look at it . . . It was something that we had always been looking for. It is wooded, it is on the lake, it was a place that we thought we could feel comfortable in as a retirement home. And so we bought it right there on the spot.

The end of the decision process was often abrupt. When the decision maker purchased a seasonal home, two events characterized the third stage of the process; finding an alternative that was judged superior to all others, and ending active search of new alternatives. For those who did not purchase, the final stage involved deciding that an attractive alternative did not exist, and ending active search.

Because the sample included people who did not buy seasonal homes, the protocols offer insight into factors that may slow or preclude purchases. The decision process may stall at any time. The next excerpt describes search activity and perception characteristic of early decision making activities, which has been going on for several years:

. . . we've looked, I mean that is kind of all part of the activity almost every summer, we do look to see what's on the market in real estate, [but] . . . I think I've learned from people that I've talked to that there is a love at first sight type of response that people have when they go to an area and they really have a great time, the weather is nice and everything works out . . . we have to sort of condition ourselves not to jump into these things on an emotional basis and when we get home and start putting the numbers on paper and checking on zoning and other kinds of things, we said well we don't know what is going to happen here in five years. And the house may fall into the lake. And, you know, there are always these things as you dig into it more deeply; the risk side of it begins to come out and the emotional love affair sort of balances out, and you say well maybe it is better just to hang on to the money and use it to rent.

Another decision maker described framing the decision and engaging in extensive search activities before deciding not to purchase:

The thought process that put us on hold financially is that ah, we are finding that everything is a lot, costs a lot more than what it used to which I know, and then five years from now it is going to cost a lot more than what it does now, too. I realize the cycle is going up, not down. And interest rates are attractive now, but you know how long that will be. And the other thing, what we did is ah, instead of, I had some equity that we were willing to make a decision on and rather than making the decision to put it into property, we've added on to our house . . . So that sort of took up that burning desire to go deeper into debt.

Some sources of delay, or time spent in the decision process when the decision maker still intends to find a seasonal home but is not actively searching, can also be identified from the protocols. One source of delay was the sequential availability of seasonal homes. When the alternatives that form the choice set are not necessarily available at the same time, the decision maker must decide whether to act on those presently available, or wait, risking the loss of a present opportunity for expected future options (Simon, 1955; Richardson, 1982). This decision maker describes waiting for future opportunities:

So then I contacted a real estate agent and gave them the parameters of what I had in mind and there just wasn't hardly anything available. . . . [But] people are always moving along. They are either upgrading or dying or something, ah, so you just have somebody watching. So anyway, why ah, I got a call that there was a place that it looked as though the contract might not go through. And so I went up and saw it and [it was] real nice, but it turned out, the contract did go through. Then a couple of others. Then [they] called me and said there was a really nice place right on the water, it fit everything that I wanted . . . but it was a good little piece of money, more than I was thinking of. So well as soon as I saw it, that was it.

Other sources of delay arose after the interviews. Approximately a year after conducting these interviews, we checked back with two subjects interviewed early in the decision process who had intended to continue their search for a seasonal home. Neither had done so. One couple decided they needed a bigger permanent home, and so stopped looking for seasonal homes. They plan to resume looking sometime next year. The other suffered major health problems and is unsure about when, if ever, he will resume searching.

DISCUSSION

The verbal protocols indicate that there are four stages decision makers pass through before making a seasonal home purchase decision (Figure 1):

- *Decision framing*, where the decision maker learns about the decision environment, makes initial resource allocations, and edits choice and criteria sets;
- *Active search*, where the decision maker visits potential seasonal homes, often working with a real estate agent,
- *Evaluation*, where the decision maker judges the desirability of the alternatives in the choice set; and
- *Resolution*, where the decision maker finds, or decides they will not be able to find, an attractive alternative, and stops searching new alternatives.

While decision makers are expected to progress through these stages in sequence, e.g, decision framing, followed by active search and evaluation, the sequence can be disrupted by changes in the decision maker's situation or in the decision environment, leading to early resolution, or to a return to an earlier stage in the process.

The protocols collected from seasonal home buyers suggest several tentative conclusions regarding complex, leisure-related purchase decisions:

1. There is great variation in individual decision processes.
2. Most decision makers are inexperienced.
3. Decisions often involve multiple decision makers.
4. Decision makers go through a series of stages.
5. The choice set is open-ended and evolves over the course of the decision process.
6. Decisions are made over an extended time period.
7. The decision process is dynamic, with extensive learning, adaptation, timelag, and feedback effects.

By combining elements of behavioral decision theory and information processing models with the findings from the protocols, we can propose a general model of the seasonal home choice process (Figure 2).

The decision frame is central to the model. The frame provides the organizational structure which directs search and evaluation activity. Non-

FIGURE 1. The Four Stages of Complex Choice.

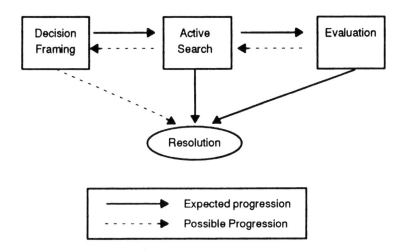

routine decisions may be defined as those for which the decision-maker lacks a readily retrievable frame. Indeed, in the seasonal home choice process, considerable time is spent in stage one simply framing the problem. Key elements of the frame for seasonal home purchases are the budget, the timeframe for completing the process, and the motivations or objectives for purchasing a seasonal home. Evaluation criteria and search strategies are also considered part of the frame.

Two sets of factors determine the structure of the decision frame: (1) characteristics of the decision maker and (2) characteristics of the decision environment. Frames can be expected to vary across individuals with different socioeconomic characteristics and previous experience. Many factors in the decision environment also influence how the seasonal home decision is framed. The structure and nature of information and information sources will be particularly important when decision makers are inexperienced. Complex decisions often require gathering information from many sources, and consideration of both present and expected future conditions. Spatial aspects of the seasonal home decision significantly complicate both search and evaluation.

Once a general decision frame is established, search and evaluation proceed in a more directed fashion. The vast majority of decision research begins here, at the "decision making behavior" box of Figure 2. Decision making behavior can be divided between search and evaluation processes, following the two primary themes in the decision literature. From this

FIGURE 2. A General Model of Complex Choice.

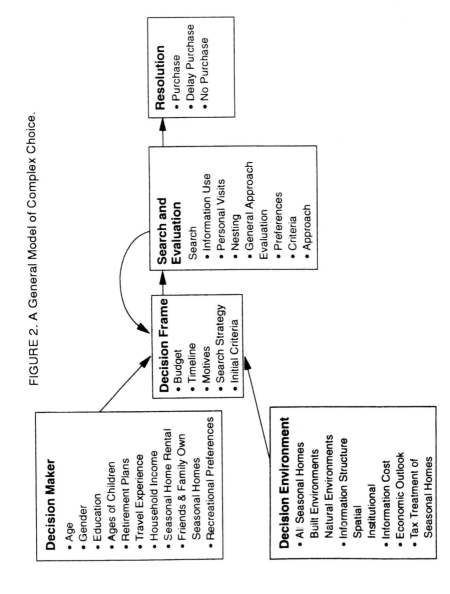

point in an atemporal, linear process, the decision maker would identify alternatives, evaluate them, and make a choice.

Extended, complex choices, however, are generally not linear. As decision makers age and learn more about themselves and the decision environment, the framing of a problem can change. For example, a person who began looking for a place to boat and relax on weekends may at some point decide she is now looking for a place to retire. Budgets, timeframes, evaluation criteria, and perceptions of the alternatives can all be revised extensively as the process continues and as time passes. Decision frames may need to be altered to make the problem solvable.

Instead of choosing among (or eliminating from) a set of given alternatives at a single point in time, a complex decision process takes place over an extended time period and may ultimately result in choice. A choice occurs when at least one satisfactory alternative is available at a time when other conditions permit the completion of a decision. The process may never end, may be postponed indefinitely, or may be resolved in a "no choice" option. Seasonal homes are relatively unique and involve both a specific property and a given location. Each alternative may only be available for a short time, adding pressure to make a decision if and when the right one appears. Both the decision maker and the decision environment can add or remove alternatives, increasing uncertainty and adding some risk to postponing a decision.

While specific frame elements and variables will be different for other complex decisions, the general processes and dynamic elements observed for seasonal homes are likely to be observed in other extended, complex decisions. Simpler choices such as those widely studied in marketing and tourism can be seen as special cases or simplifications of more general decision processes. Time is perhaps the dimension that decision researchers have most neglected, explaining the general absence of learning, adaptation, and feedback processes within decision models.

IMPLICATIONS

Marketing complex or strategic goods might be improved through attention to the unique nature of complex choice. The concept of relationship marketing and its emphasis on maintaining contact with the customer and understanding and adapting to their needs and wants has special relevance for complex choice (Levitt, 1983; Mahoney & Warnell, nd.). Providing information, assistance, personal contacts and other services which are tailored to the decision maker's stage in the choice process could help both the customer and the vendor. During decision framing, the buyer needs information about the class of goods or alternatives in general, and about expedient methods of searching alternatives. During search and evaluation, the buyer will be most open to receiving specific information about a given alternative. Once the buyer reaches the evaluation stage, maintaining contact becomes essential in order to identify and capitalize on the buyer's readiness to resolve the decision process.

The importance of decision framing in complex choice, together with the prevalence of strategic and complex decisions related to tourism has implications for conducting tourism choice research. Understanding how people frame tourism decisions would allow researchers to present subjects with choices that utilize frames like their own, improving the validity of decision experiments. The extent of individual variation in decision making, which appears to be amplified by decision complexity and duration, makes reliance on a single choice model problematic. Because of their proposed link to decision behavior, decision frames could be a useful tool for segmenting decision makers into groups, allowing distinct structural models to be developed for each.

REFERENCES

Abelson, R.P. & Levi, A. 1985. Decision making and decision theory. *In*: G. Lindzey and E. Aronson, (eds.), *The Handbook of Social Psychology* (3rd ed.) Vol.1. (pp. 231-309). New York: Random House.

Arndt, J. 1976. Reflections on research in consumer behavior. *Advances in Consumer Research 3*: 213-221.

Auriat, N. 1993. "My wife knows best": A comparison of event dating accuracy between the wife, the husband, the couple, and the Belgium population register. *Public Opinion Quarterly 57*:165-190.

Bettman, J.R., Johnson, E., & Payne, J.W. 1991. Consumer decision making. *In*: Robertson, T.S. & Kassarjian, H.H. (eds.) *Handbook of Consumer Behavior.* (pp. 50-84). Engelwood Cliffs, N.J.: Prentice Hall.

Bradburn, N., Rips, L., & Shevell, S. 1987. Answering autobiographical questions: the impact of memory and inference on surveys. *Science 236*: 157-161.

Edwards, W. 1961. Behavioral decision theory. *Annual Review of Psychology 12*: 473-498.

Einhorn, H.J. & Hogarth, R.M. 1981. Behavioral decision theory: Processes of judgement and choice. *Annual Review of Psychology 32*: 53-88.

_____. 1985. *A Contrast/Surprise Model for Updating Beliefs*. Center for Decision Research, Graduate School of Business, The University of Chicago.

Ericsson, K.A. & Simon, H.A. 1984. *Protocol analysis: Verbal reports as data.* Cambridge, MA: The MIT Press.

Ford, K., Schmitt, N., Schechtman, S., Hults, B. & Doherty, M. 1989. Process tracing methods: Contributions, problems, and neglected research questions. *Organizational Behavior and Human Decision Processes 43*: 75-117.

Goodrich, J.N. 1978. The relationship between preferences for and perceptions of vacation destinations: Application of a choice model. *Journal of Travel Research 17* (Fall): 8-13.

Gredal, K. 1966. Purchasing behavior in households *In*: Max Kjaer-Hanson (ed.), *Readings in Danish Consumer Theory of Marketing*. Kobenhavn: Einar Harcks Forlag.

Haider, W., & Ewing, G.O. 1990. A model of tourist choices of hypothetical Caribbean destinations. *Leisure Sciences 12*: 33-47.

Haines. 1974. Process models of consumer decision making. *In*: Hughes, G.D. and Ray, M.L. (eds.), *Buyer/Consumer Decision Making*. Chapel Hill: The University of North Carolina Press.

Hammond, K.R., McClelland, G.H., and Mumpower, J. 1980. *Human judgement and decision making: Theories, methods, and procedures*. New York: Praeger.

Hogarth, R.M. 1986. Generalization in decision research: The role of formal models. *IEEE Transaction on Systems, Man, and Cybernetics, vol. SMC-16, no. 3*: 439-449.

Kahneman, D. & Tversky, A. 1979. Prospect theory: An analysis of decisions under risk. *Econometrica 47*: 263-291.

Levitt, T. 1983. *The Marketing Imagination*. New York: Free Press.

Lieber, S.R. and Fesenmaier, D. 1984. Modelling recreation choice: A case study of management alternatives in Chicago. *Regional Studies 18*: 31-43.

Louviere, J. 1983. Integrating conjoint and functional measurement with discrete choice theory: An experimental design approach. *Advances in Consumer Research 10*: 151-156.

Louviere, J. 1988. *Analyzing decision making: Metric conjoint analysis*. Sage university paper series on Quantitative Applications in the Social Sciences, Series No.07-001. Beverly Hills: Sage.

Louviere, J. & Timmermans, H. 1990a. Stated preference and choice models applied to recreation: A review. *Leisure Sciences 12*:9-32.

Louviere, J. & Timmermans, H. 1990b. Using hierarchical information integration to model consumer response to possible planning actions: A recreation destination choice illustration. *Environment and Planning, A 22*: 291-308.

McFadden, D. 1978. Modeling the choice of residential location. *In*: A. Karlquist et al. (eds.), *Spatial Interaction: Theory and Planning Methods* (pp.75-96). Amsterdam: North Holland.

Mahoney, E. & Warnell, G. *Quality Assurance and the Need for a More Comprehensive Customer Oriented Approach to Service*. East Lansing, MI: Travel, Tourism, & Recreation Resource Center, Michigan State University.

Newell, A., Shaw, J.C., & Simon, H.A. 1958. Elements of a theory of human problem solving. *Psychology Review 65*: 151-166.

Newell, A. & Simon, P. 1972. *Human Problem Solving*. Englewood Cliffs, NJ: Prentice-Hall.

Nisbett, R.E. & Ross, L. 1980. *Human Inference: Strategies and Shortcomings of Social Judgment*. Englewood Cliffs, NJ: Prentice-Hall.

Richardson, A. 1982. Search models and choice set generation. *Transportation Research, 16 A* (5-6): 403-419.

Robinson, J.A. 1976. Sampling autobiographical memory. *Cognitive Psychology* 8(4): 578-595.

Rubin, D. (ed.). 1986. *Autobiographical memory.* Cambridge: Cambridge University Press.

Silberstein, A. 1989. Recall effects in the U.S. consumer expenditure interview study. *Journal of Official Statistics 5*(2): 125-142.

Simon, H.A. 1955. A behavioral model of rational choice. *Quarterly Journal of Economics 69*: 99-118.

Strauss, A. & Corbin, J. 1990. *Basics of Qualitative Research.* Newbury Park, CA: Sage.

Stynes, D.J. & Peterson, G. 1984. A review of logit models with implications for modeling recreation choices. *Journal of Leisure Research 16*(4): 295-310.

Tversky, A. 1972. Elimination by aspects: A theory of choice. *Psychological Review 79* (4): 281-298.

Tversky, A. & Kahneman, D. 1974. Judgement under uncertainty: Heuristics and biases. *Science 185* (Sept.): 1124-1131.

Um, S., & Crompton, J. 1990. Attitude determinants in tourism destination choice. *Annals of Tourism Research 17*: 432-448.

Vining, J. & Fishwick, L. 1991. An exploratory study of outdoor recreation site choices. *Journal of Leisure Research 23*(2): 114-132.

External Information Search:
Effects of Tour Brochures
with Experiential Information

Cees F. Goossens

SUMMARY. External information sources are employed by tourists and form the basis for vacation planning. For marketers it is relevant to know what kind of information should be used in tour brochures to stimulate the tourist's external vacation search process. In this context the effect of experiential and non-experiential information on external search behavior is examined in a field experiment. External information search is defined as the request of a free vacation magazine through the sending of a brochure response card. Actually, this overt behavioral response to brochures is measured as the dependent variable. The results indicate that tour brochures with experiential texts and a readers' instruction to enactive imagery, did not cause more external search than brochures without such information.

GATHERING TOURIST INFORMATION

The problems of tourism marketing are different from the problems of traditional product marketing. The differences are the result of the characteristics of tourism supply and demand. Tourism is a *service*. An intangible

Cees F. Goossens is Assistant Professor of Psychology and Marketing at the Department for Leisure Studies, Tilburg University. P.O. Box 90153, 5000 LE Tilburg, The Netherlands.

[Haworth co-indexing entry note]: "External Information Search: Effects of Tour Brochures with Experiential Information." Cees F. Goossens. Co-published simultaneously in the *Journal of Travel & Tourism Marketing* (The Haworth Press, Inc.) Vol. 3, No. 3, 1994, pp. 89-107; and: *Economic Psychology of Travel and Tourism* (ed: John C. Crotts, and W. Fred van Raaij), The Haworth Press, Inc., 1994, pp. 89-107. Multiple copies of this article/chapter may be purchased from The Haworth Document Delivery Center [1-800-3-HAWORTH; 9:00 a.m. - 5:00 p.m. (EST)].

89

experience is being sold, not a physical good that can be inspected prior to purchase (Mill and Morrison, 1985). Generalizations that have widespread acceptance among scholars and practitioners in the field as being characteristic of services include intangibility, simultaneity of production and consumption and nonstandardization (see Zeithaml, Parasuraman, and Berry, 1985). Services are not directly perceptible and are unpredictable in their outcomes for the buyer. This implies that they would influence purchasing behavior of consumers. These fundamental characteristics of services appear to create particular uncertain and risky purchase situations. In this context, Murray (1991) states that it is logical to expect that consumers acquire information as a strategy of risk reduction in the face of this specific uncertainty. Moreover he argues that services are more difficult to evaluate than goods. As a consequence, consumers may be forced to rely on other cues and processes when evaluating services.

Tourism marketers may benefit from the improved knowledge of *search behavior* in vacation planning. In general, knowledge of information acquisition strategies is important to marketing managers because information search is at an early influential stage in the purchase decision process. In fact, the information sources employed by tourists form the basis for vacation planning (Van Raaij and Francken, 1984). Consumer information sources can be classified into two broad types, internal and external; both types are used by consumers to gather information and cope with perceived risk. This article focuses on *external* information search regarding vacations.

In this field of research information importance is a significant determinant of both prepurchase and ongoing external search. Furthermore, ongoing external search and the balance of prepurchase to ongoing search activities are also influenced by enduring involvement and previous experience (see Perdue, 1993). In general, sources of external information search can be classified in terms of whether the source is marketing oriented or whether information comes from personal or impersonal communication (Engel, Blackwell, and Miniard, 1986). Non-marketer-dominated information sources such as personal media are expected to play a particularly important role in the consumer decision process for services. However, personal information sources and mass media are related in several ways. For example, tourism research indicates that mass media (such as touristic advertising and brochures) are consulted most in the beginning, and personal media (such as salespersons, friends, personal advice) are mainly used at a latter stage of the vacation planning (van Raaij and Francken, 1984).

Tour brochures and other sources of mass media initially play a significant role in determining choice of recreation and vacation destinations. Because consumers understand that the purpose of these mass media is to persuade as well as to inform, they discount the value of this 'biased' information and seek to verify its authenticity (see Maute and Forrester, 1991). This phenomenon is reflected in the fact that people in the vacation group usually share in the information search process, and often several sources of information are consulted in planning a trip. In general, the vacation search process involves one or more individuals along with a variety of sources for a multiple set of decisions (see, e.g., Capella and Greco, 1987; Nichols and Snepenger, 1988; Snepenger et al., 1990). With regard to vacation decision making it is found that social information sources are the most important. Members of the immediate family rank first, relatives second, and friends third (Jenkins, 1978). These facts are in line with Murray's (1991) conclusion that service consumers prefer the opinions and experiences of other comparable individuals in making service purchase decisions.

Vacations are intangibles, which means that the prospective buyer can neither see or feel them prior to purchase, nor can he return the product if he is dissatisfied. Mansfeld (1992) states that tourism marketers should follow two prevailing research strategies. One is the study of tourists' stated preferences; the other is the study of actual choice. He suggests that the second research direction should look into the information gathering stage. In this case, the impact of promotional information material on touristic choice behavior should be examined. Because this material is meant to create favorable images and to stimulate "nonleading" motivations, it is important to evaluate its "bias effect" on possible choice directions. More specifically Perdue (1993, p. 184) states that research focusing on propensity to seek information as a dependent variable, particularly within the context of the growing body of hedonic consumption literature, may significantly improve external search theory, and distinguishing between the decision or propensity to seek information and the actual selection and use of alternative sources of information may significantly improve our theoretical understanding of external search behavior.

BROCHURES

Leisure studies demonstrate that tourists rely more on informational material while preparing their trip at home than after arriving at their destination (Mansfeld, 1992). In this context Manfredo (1989) points at the fact that so called 'active information seekers' (i.e., individuals who are deliberately searching for external information) are of particular interest because of the possibility that they are ready to act (e.g., visit a given area) and because they may be susceptible to persuasive appeals. When we keep in mind that tourists prefer personal information, it is reasonable to assume that persuasive communication strategies should stress experiential or subjective rather than technical or objective dimensions of the trips on offer. This means that travel agencies and tour operators should make the vacation more tangible in brochures by providing visible or explanatory cues that prospective tourists can use to evaluate the ultimate (emotional) advantages and quality of the vacation. Potential inclusive tour buyers, although they can bear in mind word-of-mouth and published recommendations as well as their own past personal experience, still have to rely largely on what they read and see in operators' brochures; the tour brochure is therefore a key sales tool for the tour operator. Interestingly enough, tour operators' brochures have many similarities with commercial published leisure magazines. They are regarded by their users as being "a good read," whetting the appetite for the vacation products on offer (see Hodgson, 1990). From this hedonic and motivational point of view it is important to stress *experiential information* in brochures. Promotional leisure information about feelings of pleasure, relaxation, excitement, adventure and fun probably will motivate tourists to plan a trip.

Actually there is no scientific study available in the travel research and destination marketing literature on whether advertising stimulates tourism (see Woodside, 1990). While tourism 'advertising conversions research' studies (e.g., Woodside and Soni, 1988) are helpful in comparing the performance of different ads, media vehicles, and media, such advertising conversion studies do not address the more basic question like: What kind of information should be used in brochures to trigger the external search behavior of tourists?

Since tour brochures are infrequently effective in getting the attention of the information seeker, it is useful to examine the impact of different types of brochure-information on external search behavior. In particular the present article will test two hypotheses regarding 'external search' effectiveness of brochures. The communication strategy focuses on increasing people's response when given the opportunity to request free information about coast vacations in the Netherlands. In this context a field experiment is reported that tests the effect of tour brochures with pictures and 'experiential texts' on external search behavior. The theoretical and practical implications for tour brochures are discussed.

MENTAL IMAGERY AND BEHAVIORAL INTENTIONS

In general, consumer researchers suggest that the experiential aspects of consumption play an important role in consumer choice behavior (see Hirschman and Holbrook, 1982; Holbrook and Hirschman, 1982). From this point of view, MacInnis and Price (1987) state that in the choice of many leisure services an important part of the choice involves assessing how it will feel (the sensation surrounding the anticipated leisure experience). Regarding the latter, experiential processes, such as imagining, daydreams, and emotions, play an important role in vacation choice behavior (see Mannell and Iso-Ahola, 1987). In this perspective, it is reasonable to assume that when consumers imagine touristic behavior they direct their attention on desirable feelings and leisure experiences. It is self-evident that other, more economic and rational, aspects of holidays will be regarded too (e.g., modes of travelling, accommodation and expense), but these non-emotional aspects are beyond the scope of this paper.

MacInnis and Price (1987) provide several propositions about the potentially unique effects of elaborated imagery on consumer behavior, such as the stimulating influence of elaborated imagery on affective experiences, purchase intentions, and purchase timing. This relationship between elaborated imagery and enhanced purchase desire is directly relevant to a promotional strategy that focuses on stimulating external search behavior. Evidence suggests that imagery-producing ads result in superior recall and more positive attitudes toward the product. However, there has been limited examination of the relationship between imagery and behavioral intentions in a marketing context. Only Gregory, Cialdini, and Carpenter (1982) found that individuals who were asked to imagine themselves enjoying the benefits of cable TV, had greater intentions to subscribe to the cable service than did the individuals who were simply told about these benefits.

According to Aylwin (1990), adults can use three different though interconnected forms of representation: verbal representation, or inner speech; visual imagery, or 'pictures in the mind's eye'; and enactive imagery, a kind of imagined action or role play. Enactive imagery is specialized for representing the temporal and affective aspects of a stimulus. This temporal perspective of enactive imagery extends to include the possible consequences of action. Enactive imagery provides an insider's perspective on situations, and allows access to subjective aspects opaque to subjects using verbal or visual representations. Aylwin (1990) states that affective and other subjective constructs are most frequent in enactive imagery. This fact is in line with Lang's (1984) work, which shows that representations involving active participation are accompanied by more affective arousal (as indexed by physiological indices such as heart rate) than purely visual representations.

Actually, enactive imagery is a form of cognitive representation in which the consumer is personally involved with stimuli, through "do-it-yourself or experience-it-yourself" thoughts (see Goossens, 1994). This conceptualisation of enactive imagery is comparable with the concept of 'self-relatedness' (see Anderson, 1983; Bone and Ellen, 1990) and Krugman's conception of high involvement. Krugman (1965) suggested that at the highest level of involvement consumers produce "personal connections," or "bridging experiences," whereby they relate the ad content to meaningful aspects of their own life. Furthermore enactive imagery is narrow related to the concept "constructive processing." Here, the consumer goes beyond the ad's content and connects it in some meaningful way to his or her own life. Examples of these constructive elaborations include thinking up novel uses for the product and/or imagining the product in use (see MacInnis and Jaworski, 1989; Buchholz and Smith, 1991).

Bone and Ellen (1990) reported a study which provides a stimulating contribution to the knowledge of the effect of imagery processing and imagery content on behavioral intentions. Based on the study of Anderson (1983), they empirically examined the relationship between self-related imagery and behavioral intentions in a radio advertising context. In this experiment radio was selected as the experimental medium because self-generated imagery should have a greater effect than other-generated imagery. If a consumer is forced to create his/her own images, the mental processing is at a deeper level than if the images are created for him/her (e.g., through pictures). In their study Bone and Ellen (1990) found support for the hypothesis that self-related imagery creates more positive behavioral intentions than other-related imagery. Given the results of this self-relatedness factor, it appears that consumer researchers may wish to investigate other message characteristics, such as promotional texts with hedonic information, which could directly or indirectly affect behavioral intentions when imagery processing occurs.

HYPOTHESES

A characteristic of the medium 'tour brochure' is that pictures are used to generate mental imagery processing and emotional experiences. In this context it is relevant for tour operators to investigate the effect of the use of self-related imagery-instructions and verbal emotional information on external search behavior. To be effective in stimulating the external information search of tourists, persuasive communication strategies need to focus on helping persons to imagine the positive sensory and emotional experiences of vacations. From this point of view the tourism industry should use emotional information in their promotion campaigns. By using information about feelings of pleasure and fun, advertisers actually try to tempt the consumer to plan a trip. Regarding the latter, the purpose of this paper is to test two hypotheses.

H1: Tour brochures with a reader's instruction to enactive imagery processing, and the presentation of experiential texts will cause more external information search than brochures without such information.

This hypothesis is supported by a the next proposition: 'The greater the use of cues that appeal to hedonic needs, the greater consumers' motivation to attend to the ad' (see MacInnis, Moorman and Jaworski, 1991). Apart from verbal information, figural/prominent stimuli can be used to enhance the attention to tour brochures. Research indicates a strong impact of pictures on attention, elaboration, and memory. Moreover the size of the ad itself influences ad prominence and consequent attention to the ad (Finn, 1988). Based on this literature a second hypothesis is developed regarding visual information (i.e., picture size):

H2: Brochures with large pictures will cause more information search than brochures with small pictures.

This hypothesis is supported by the next proposition: 'The greater the use of figural/prominent executional cues, the greater consumers' motivation to attend to the ad' (see MacInnis, Moorman and Jaworski, 1991). Because of the widespread use of pictures in tour brochures, knowing the effect of picture size on all kind of dependent variables (such as attitude toward the ad, behavioral intentions, and overt behavioral responses) is of considerable importance to tour brochure design. In this context H2 is explorative.

METHODOLOGY

In 1991 the Netherlands Board for Tourism and the Department for Leisure Studies (Tilburg University) performed a field experiment. The main purpose of this project was to measure the effects of brochures with experiential texts and large pictures on external information search. To test the hypotheses a 2 × 2 factorial design was used. The *independent* variables were types of verbal information and picture size. The *dependent* variable 'external information search' is defined as the request for a free vacation magazine by returning a response card. So, in this field experiment the overt behavioral response of an individual is measured as the dependent variable. In this context the present experiment tests whether the type of brochure information affects the request of a free magazine. Brochures with enactive imagery instructions, experiential texts and large pictures are supposed to be more attractive and will increase the return of the response card. Brochures without experiential texts and small pictures will have a smaller impact.

BROCHURE CHARACTERISTICS

To test the hypotheses, four types of coast brochures are developed. These brochures describe vacation situations and are identical in outline, except for the type of verbal information and picture size. In fact the differentiation between the four brochure types is as follows:

1. Experiential texts and Large pictures   (= brochure EL)
2. Experiential texts and Small pictures   (= brochure ES)
3. Non-experiential texts and Large pictures (= brochure NL)
4. Non-experiential texts and Small pictures (= brochure NS)

Each brochure type consists of four pages. The front cover contains three pictures and a slogan. The slogan with emotional information is "Enjoy a trip in your own country," whereas the slogan without experiential information runs as follows "Make a trip in your own country."

The back cover describes the possibility to get additional information about the Dutch coast, and a response card to request the free coast magazine. In the 'emotional' brochures the text is completed with experiential aspects of consumer behavior in the vacation planning stage, such as "Set out to discover how attractive our country is!"

The other two pages contain six pictures with captions. The manipulation of the so called experiential information in these captions is as follows: In the 'emotional' brochures (EL and ES) the reader is instructed to imagine the vacation situations. According to MacInnis and Price (1987, p. 485) imagery instructions may be an important manipulation strategy when consumers are allowed the time to generate vivid imagery, when cues are concrete, when instructions focus on subjects' reactions to the image, and when consumers have sufficient knowledge to generate imagery about reactions. Since the coast is a well-known vacation destination for the Dutch, this study meets the latter requirement. Moreover the six pictures can be conceived as concrete cues.

To describe the vacation situations as realistically as possible, concrete words are used which describe the vacation situation. Moreover the behavioral situation is completed with descriptions of leisure feelings. An exclamation point (!) is used to stress this verbal information. To facilitate that subjects' will personally engage in enactive imagery processing, all experiential texts contain the word "you." According to these criteria the caption of the first picture is as follows: "Glorious relaxation on the Dutch beaches . . . than you will really settle down! These manipulation criteria are missing in the brochures with non-experiential texts (*NL* and *NS*). For example, the first picture caption runs simply "The Dutch beaches."

BROCHURE DISTRIBUTION

In April 1991 20,000 brochures were distributed by a professional direct mail agency in Tilburg (Tilburg is a semi-large city in The Netherlands, about 100 kilometers from the Dutch west coast). To test the effect of the brochure types on coupon response 5,000 brochures of each type were distributed. The selection of the 20,000 addresses was based on postcode areas. The selection criteria were; an equal distribution of social class, in the better neighbourhoods, and primarily houses with gardens. The distribution of the four brochure types was random. That is, the brochures were delivered from door to door (i.e., direct non mail) and in a mixed order (i.e., *EL, NL, ES, NS, EL,* . . . etc.). Owing to the large number of subjects, it is supposed that possible intervening factors, such as the individual characteristics of the subjects, are the same in the four brochure groups. The brochures each contains a *response card* with which the potential tourists can request free information about Dutch coast vacations. These cards are unobstrusively marked with the corresponding brochure codes *EL, NL, ES,* and *NS*.

RESULTS

One thousand two hundred eighty-three subjects (6.4%) returned the response card. To investigate how brochure characteristics affect the response rates (see H1 and H2), the response numbers have been examined across the four cell conditions. Table 1 reports these rates.

A chi-square analysis (on contingency tables) is performed to investi-

TABLE 1: Response card rates across brochure types.

Brochure type	Response yes	no	
EL	330	4,670	5,000
NL	328	4,672	5,000
ES	300	4,700	5,000
NS	325	4,675	5,000
Total	1,283	18,717	20,000

Chi-square value = 1.95
Critical chi-square value = 7.82 (α = .05; df = 3)

gate the effects of 'type of verbal information' and 'picture size' on response rate. The overall chi-square with three degrees of freedom equals 1.95. The critical chi-square value equals 7.82 (α = .05; df = 3), this means that the brochure characteristics do not affect the redemption rates. In other words, the response rates are equally divided among the four brochure groups. Although these results do not support H1 and H2, it may be possible that the brochure characteristics affect the *response time* of the subjects. Perhaps emotional brochures cause a faster response.

For this analysis the returned cards were dated on the day of entrance (the date-line was end May). To investigate the effect of brochure characteristics on response time, the subjects are divided into two categories: *(1)* Subjects with a *fast* response time (date of entry, 1-3 May). *(2)* Subjects with a *slow* response time (date of entry, 6-31 May). So we speak of a subject with a fast response time, when she/he returned the response card during the same week in which the brochures were distributed. Table 2 reports the response time per brochure type.

A chi-square analysis (on contingency tables) is performed to investigate the effects of 'type of verbal information' and 'picture size' on response time. The overall chi-square with three degrees of freedom equals 5.24. The critical chi-square value equals 7.82 (α = .05; df = 3), this means that the two response time categories are equally divided among the four brochure types.

A chi-square analysis (on a 2 × 2 crosstable; see Table 3) is performed to investigate the effect of 'type of verbal information' on 'response time.'

TABLE 2: Response time per brochure type.

| Response time | Brochure type | | | | |
	EL	NL	ES	NS	
Fast	218	209	189	230	846
Slow	112	119	111	95	437
Total	330	328	300	325	1,283

Chi-square value = 5.24
Critical chi-square value = 7.82 (α = .05; df = 3)

TABLE 3: Response card rates and the relation between response time and type of verbal information.

| Response time | Verbal information | | |
	Emotional	Non-emotional	
Fast	407	439	846
Slow	223	214	437
Total	630	653	1,283

Chi-square value = 0.98 (before Yates correction)
Critical chi-square value = 3.84 (α = .05; df = 1)

The overall chi-square with one degree of freedom equals 0.98 (before Yates correction). The critical chi-square value equals 3.84 (α = .05; df = 1), this means that brochures with emotional information do not affect the response time.

A chi-square analysis (on a 2×2 crosstable; see Table 4) is performed to investigate the effect of 'picture size' on 'response time.' The overall chi-square with one degree of freedom equals 0.66 (before Yates correction). The critical chi-square value equals 3.84 (α = .05; df = 1), this means that brochures with large pictures do not affect the response time.

TABLE 4: Response card rates and the relation between response time and picture size.

	Picture size		
	Large	Small	
Response time			
Fast	427	419	846
Slow	231	206	437
Total	658	625	1,283

Chi-square value = 0.66 (before Yates correction)
Critical chi-square value = 3.84 (α = .05; df = 1)

MANIPULATION CHECK

The field experimental results do not support H1 and H2, besides the brochure types did not affect the subjects' response time. Regarding this, the four brochure types were post-tested in a manipulation check (see Goossens, 1992). In an experimental design 76 subjects evaluated the brochure types on a questionnaire. Per brochure type the number of subjects were: ES n = 20, NS n = 19, EL n = 18, and NL n = 19. Several independent variables were measured, such as sex, age and previous experience with coast vacations. A between-subjects factorial design was used (i.e., Type of Information/Picture Size/Sex). In this context several dependent variables were measured on 7 point scales, such as the brochure attractiveness, imagery processing, and the 'felt-involvement' with the coast brochure (for more information about the 'felt-involvement' concept the reader is referred to Celsi and Olson, 1988).

The major results of the conducted ANOVA's indicate that both experiential texts and large pictures did not affect the attractiveness of the cover and the overall information provided in the brochures. Besides, the emotional texts did not affect the degree to which the subjects could project themselves into the experience of the vacation situation (i.e., enactive imagery). There is reason to assume that a stated level of low involvement with the particular touristic information explains the unexpected results. On the other hand, it is possible that mere descriptive (verbal) experiential information is not effective in making brochures more attractive. This may be explained by the fact that people tend to respond to advertising with, what van Raaij (1984) calls, a primary affective reaction. Furthermore he assumes that a cognitive elaboration of information does not change the first impression of an ad. According to van Raaij this phenomenon is especially valid for visual information. In this perspective Goossens (1993) argues that vacation pictures with people who express their positive feelings visually will have a positive effect on the attractiveness of touristic brochures. Moreover visual information about emotional experiences, such as facial expressions of positive feelings, are cues which probably improve the consumer's motivation to attend to an ad.

DISCUSSION

In the present study only the external search response on 20,000 brochures was measured. For practical reasons it was impossible to measure the subjects' mode of information processing in the large field experiment. So, we do not know whether the respondents used their imagination or not. Regarding this the next discussion will be based on relevant imagery literature.

The unexpected results can be explained by the fact that the four brochure types probably triggered the same extent mental imagery processing. This explanation is supported by the results of the manipulation check. In this case the emotional brochures (*EL* and *ES*) did not provoke more enactive imagery and positive affect than the so called non-emotional brochures (*NL* and *NS*). In addition it turned out that the subjects' level of felt-involvement with the brochure types was the same.

Why the emotional brochure types did not affect the coupon response can be explained by the fact that all brochure types were primarily pictorial. This means that the images were already created for the subjects. Indeed, Bone and Ellen (1990) found a positive relationship between self-related imagery processing and behavioral intentions, however they forced the subjects to create their own images by using radio advertisements as medium. Gregory et al. (1982) found the same imagery effect on behavioral intentions, but also in this study the subjects processed just verbal information. More recently Buchholz and Smith (1991) found that when consumers are involved, radio was shown to produce significantly more personal elaboration than TV commercials.

Probably imagery instructions and experiential texts are only effective in brochures without pictures. Regarding this, it is necessary to know which factors stimulate imagery processing, so that these variables can be manipulated in brochures to improve external information search. In this context the next suggestions for future laboratory research are useful: In general, imagery processing is often used by consumers to evaluate marketing stimuli, and consumers differ with respect to their ability and desire to invoke imagery processes. Imagery may potentially improve the believability and memorability of a communication and influence consumer processing and responses. The understanding how individuals differ in their abilities to process imagery in various *senses* (see Gutman, 1988), and how use of enactive imagery influences the way consumers evaluate tour brochures, may help identify more effective ways to reach active vacation information seekers.

Special needs for services advertising to tangiblize the intangible offering, make a complex product clear to the consumer, and differentiate one brand from another are shown to relate to figurative language use. Regarding this Stern (1988) argues that creative and symbolic language may be used to endow the abstract service with *sense appeal*, and an analysis of figures of speech can help advertisers determine which kinds will most effectively reach consumers. However, the exact nature of emotional responses to advertising is only beginning to be investigated (see Zeitlin and Westwood, 1986), and the relationship of verbal and pictorial symbolic usage to effects of feelings on consumer responses needs further examination to a service context. MacInnis and Price (1990), and Bone and Ellen (1990) reported explorative studies which provide stimulating contributions to the knowledge of imagery processing. According to Hughes (1990) a problem of these studies is that they are focused on a static concept, namely recalled processed information, and not on the dynamics of imagery processing. Regarding the latter, Hughes suggests that studies on imagery need realtime research measures while the subjects are processing the information. This realtime research is promising for those who are testing the effects of brochure characteristics on enactive imagery processing in laboratory experiments.

CONCLUSION

The major purpose of this field experiment was to test the effect of hedonistic advertising on external search behavior. In communication messages emotional information is often used to draw the attention of the target group, to intensify their interest, and to communicate the essence of the message. These three functions of emotions in information processing are essential for advertising goals. This study, however, was primarily focused on another function of emotion in ads, namely the motivational or behavior-activating function. In this context it was supposed that imagery instructions and the processing of verbal information about feelings should stimulate external search behavior. However, the empirical results did not support the hypotheses. This can be explained by the fact that in all brochures types the pictorial information was the same. Probably behavioral responses to touristic information are largely determined by visual impressions. In other words, the type of verbal information seems to be irrelevant. Besides, the results of the manipulation check demonstrated that all subjects reported the same levels of affect and involvement with the brochure types. Nevertheless, considerable research suggests that advertising executional cues may influence communication effectiveness. Related research indicates that communication effectiveness is in part driven by consumers' motivation to process information from an ad. However, little research has explicitly linked executional cues to communication effectiveness via their impact on motivation and levels of processing. In this perspective several propositions are relevant to future research, such as: 'The greater the use of visual cues that appeal to hedonic needs, the greater consumers' motivation to attend to the ad,' and 'The greater the use of visual cues that enhance the relevance of the vacation activities to the self, the greater consumers' motivation to process information from the ads.' Both propositions demonstrate that consumer researchers can apply the concept 'enactive imagery' in experimental designs with manipulated visual information (see Goossens, 1994). In this context the hypotheses H1 and H2 may be tested again. Follow-up research is relevant because touristic organizations usually communicate with their target groups in an emotional manner, for example by using hedonic and sensoric information in brochures, magazines, advertisements, and so on. An important part of this information concerns the consumption experience of leisure products. If the suggested hypotheses are correct and information about feelings of pleasure, relaxation, excitement, adventure and fun, meets consumers' hedonic needs, advertising may motivate tourists with adequate pictures of travellers who express their satisfactory (leisure) feelings.

The marketing implications of knowledge of search processing are diverse. For example, insight into search processes may assist in determining whether segmenting the audience may improve the efficiency of media communications. Knowledge of search processes may aid in the development of advertising appeals targeted at specific segments. Knowledge of search processes may also help to select appropriate marketing strategies for different market segments. Besides, knowledge of *external information search* may be quite useful in improving informational campaigns. Various types of customer analyses identifying individuals' search behavior have been used in tourism market planning (see, e.g., Schul and Crompton, 1983; Manfredo, 1989; Purdue, 1993). In particular Havitz and Dimanche

(1989) suggested that the relationship of the 'involvement' construct with search behavior and promotional stimuli is relevant in tourism contexts. In addition, Bloch, Sherrell and Rigdway (1986) noted that search behavior is not always limited to prepurchase events. Individuals engaging in 'ongoing search' focus more on the recreational and enjoyment value of the search than on its informational value. This so called 'ongoing search' concept is strongly related to 'enduring involvement.' In this case consumers gather information as a goal itself. This means that the satisfaction (reward) stems from engaging in the search process itself. Thus, 'ongoing searchers' are primarily intrinsically motivated for (leisure) information, which means that the search process can be seen as an activity for its own sake, or even as a specific facet of their leisure-life-style. For direct marketers such consumers are important with respect to 'word-of-mouth information' to other customers. In this context Murray's (1991) study is relevant, because his research results confirm the hypothesis that personal independent sources of information (e.g., word-of-mouth information) are more effective for services than for goods. Influence exerted by those sources appears to confirm service marketing theory, which suggests that consumers desire subjective and experiential information. On the other hand, a consumer's information search activity may be mainly extrinsically motivated, which means that the activity is satisfying in terms of its consequences or payoffs. In fact these information seekers are of particular interest for direct marketers because they may be susceptible to the emotional benefits of hedonic appeals. Considerably more research is needed to develop communication strategies that *stimulate vacation search behavior.* Touristic mass media, such as tour brochures play especially in the beginning of the vacation planning process a significant role in determining choice of destinations. Since brochures are manageable sales tools for tourism marketers, more research should be done on the effects of different kinds of verbal and visual information on vacation search behavior. Continued research along these lines will aid advertisers and media planners in their efforts to stimulate tourism.

REFERENCES

Anderson, C. A. (1983), Imagination and Expectation: The effect of Imagining Behavioral Scripts on Personal Intentions, *Journal of Personality and Social Psychology*, 45 (2), 293-305.

Aylwin, S. (1990), Imagery and Affect: Big Questions, Little Answers, in: P.J. Hampson, D.F. Marks, & J.T.E. Richardson (Eds.), *Imagery: Current Developments*; International Library of Psychology (pp. 247-67). Routledge, London and New York.

Bone, P., & Ellen, P. (1990), The Effect of Imagery Processing and Imagery Content on Behavioral Intentions, *Advances in Consumer Research*, 17, 449-454.

Bloch, P.H., Scherrell, D. & Ridgway, N. (1986), Consumer Search: An extended framework, *Journal of Consumer Research*, 13, 119-126

Buchholz, L. M. & Smith, R.E. (1991), The Role of Consumer Involvement in determining Cognitive Response to Broadcast Advertising, *Journal of Advertising*, 20, 1, 4-17.

Capella, L.M., & Greco A.J. (1987), Information Sources of Elderly for Vacation Decisions, *Annals of Tourism Research*, 14, 148-51.

Celsi, R.I. & Olson, J.C. (1988), The role of involvement in attention and comprehension processes, *Journal of Consumer Research*, 15, 210-224.

Engel, J.F., Blackwell, R.D., & Miniard, P.W. (1986), *Consumer Behavior*, New York: Dryden Press.

Finn, A. (1988), Print ad recognition Readership scores: An Information Processing Perspective, *Journal of Marketing Research*, 25 (May), 168-77.

Goossens, C.F. (1992), The effect of emotional information in touristic promotion: An evaluation of Dutch coast brochures, *Massacommunicatie*, 3, 183-211 (in Dutch).

Goossens, C.F. (1993), *Picturing a Holiday: A Study on Effects of Emotional Information*, Doctoral Dissertation, Tilburg University, The Netherlands.

Goossens, C.F. (1994), Enactive Imagery: Information Processing, Emotional Responses, and Behavioral Intentions, *Journal of Mental Imagery*.

Gregory, W.L., Cialdini, R.D., & Carpenter, K.M. (1982), "Self-Relevant Scenarios as Mediators of Likelihood Estimates and Compliance: Does Imagining Make It So," *Journal of Personality and Social Psychology*, 43, 1, 89-99.

Gutman, E. (1988), The Role of Individual Differences and Multiple Senses in Consumer Imagery Processing: Theoretical Perspectives, *Advances in Consumer Research*, 15, 191-96.

Havitz, M.E., & Dimanche, F. (1989), Propositions for Testing the Involvement Construct in Recreational and Tourism Contexts, *Leisure Sciences*, 12, 179-95.

Hirschman, E.C. & Holbrook, M.B. (1982), Hedonic Consumption: Emerging Concepts, Methods and Propositions, *Journal of Marketing*, 46 (Summer 1982), 92-101.

Hodgson, P. (1990), Using Qualitative Research to Understand Consumer Needs in Tour Brochure Design, *Travel and Tourism Research Association, 21st Annual Conference Proceedings* (October 1990).

Holbrook, M.B. & Hirschman, E.C. (1982), The experiential aspects of consumption: Consumer fantasies, feelings, and fun, *Journal of Consumer Research*, 9, 132-140.

Hughes, G. H. (1990), Studies in Imagery, Styles of Processing, and Parellel Processing Need Realtime Response Measures, *Advances in Consumer Research*, 17, 461-466.

Jenkins, R.L. (1978) Family Vacation Decision-Making, *Journal of Travel Research* 16(4):2-7.

Krugman, H.E. (1965), The Impact of Television Advertising: Learning Without Involvement, *Public Opinion Quarterly*, 29(Fall), 349-356.

Lang, P.J. (1984), Cognition in Emotion: Concept and Action. In: Izard, C., Kagan, J. & Zajonc, R. (eds.), *Emotions, Cognitions and Behavior*, New York: Cambridge University Press.

MacInnis, D.J., & Jaworski, B.J. (1989), Information Processing from Advertisements: Toward an Intergrative Framework, *Journal of Marketing*. 53 (4), 1-24.

MacInnis, D.J., Moorman, C., & Jaworski, B.J., (1991), Enhancing and Measuring Consumers' Motivation, Opportunity, and Ability to Process Brand Information From Ads, *Journal of Marketing*, 55 (October), 32-53.

MacInnis, D.J. & Price, L.L. (1987), The Role of Imagery in Information Processing: Review and Extensions, *Journal of Consumer Research*, 13, 473-491.

MacInnis, D.J. & Price, L.L. (1990), An Exploratory Study of the Effects of Imagery Processing and Consumer Experience on Expectations and Satisfaction, *Advances in Consumer Research*, 17, 41-47.

Manfredo, M.J. (1989), An Investigation of the Basis for External Information Search in Recreation and Tourism, *Leisure Sciences*, 11, 29-45.

Mannell, R.C. & Iso-Ahola, S.E. (1987), Psychological nature of leisure and tourism experience, *Annals of Tourism Research*, 14 (4), 314-331.

Mansfeld, Y. (1992), From Motivation to Travel, *Annals of Tourism Research*, 19, 399-419.

Maute, M., & Forrester, W.R. (1991), The effect of attribute qualities on consumer decision making: A causal model of external information search, *Journal of Economic Psychology*, 12, 643-666.

Mill, R.C. & Morrison, A.M. (1985), *The Tourism System: An Introductory Text*, Englewood Cliffs, N.J.: Prentice Hall.

Murray, K.B. (1991), A test of Services Marketing Theory: Consumer Information Acquisition Activities, *Journal of Marketing*, 55 (January 1991), 10-25.

Nichols, C. and D. Snepenger (1988), Family Decision Making and Tourism Behavior and Attitudes, *Journal of Travel Research*, 26 (Winter), 2-6.

Perdue, R.R. (1993), External Information Search in Marine Recreational Fishing, *Leisure Sciences*, 15, 169-187.

Schul, P. and J.L. Crompton (1983), Search Behavior of International Vacationers: Travel Specific Lifestyle and Sociodemographic Variables, *Journal of Travel Research*, 21 (Fall) 25-30.

Snepenger, D., Meged, K., Snelling, M., and Worrall K. (1990), Information Search Strategies By Destination-Naive Tourists, *Journal of Travel Research*, 28 (Summer), 13-16.

Stern, B.B. (1988), Figurative Language in Services Advertising: The Nature and Uses of Imagery, *Advances in Consumer Research*, 15, 185-90.

van Raaij, W.F. (1989), How Consumers React to Advertising, *International Journal of Advertising*, 8, 261-273.

van Raaij, W.F., & Francken, D. (1984), Vacation Decisions, Activities, and Satisfactions, *Annals of Tourism Research*, 11, 101-112.

Woodside, A. G. (1990), Measuring Advertising Effectiveness in Destination Marketing Strategies, *Journal of Travel Research*, 28 (Fall), 3-8.

Woodside, A.G., & Soni, P.K. (1988), Assessing the Quality of Advertising Inquiries by Mode of Response, *Journal of Advertising Research*, 28 (August/September), 31-37.

Zeithaml, V.A., A. Parasuraman, & Berry, L.L. (1985), Problems and Strategies in Services Marketing, *Journal of Marketing*, 49 (Spring), 33-46.

Zeitlin, D.M., & Westwood, R.A. (1986), Measuring Emotional Response, *Journal of Advertising Research*, 26 (October/November), 34-44.

Promotion and Demand
in International Tourism

Geoffrey I. Crouch

SUMMARY. The pattern of international travel and tourism demand, and its change over time, is quite pronounced. The determinants of this pattern are potentially many and varied, as evidenced by the large number of empirical studies which have been undertaken over the last three decades. Destinations attempt to influence this pattern through their promotional activities in foreign countries. Many countries have substantially increased their spending on such promotions in recent years as international tourism has become much more lucrative and competitive. However, the empirical evidence of the impact of promotion remains sketchy. Few studies have attempted to evaluate the promotional impact empirically, and those which have, have generally produced inconclusive and varied results. To investigate this variability, 197 marketing expenditure elasticities of demand from among five empirical studies were examined meta-analytically. The results indicate that there exists an underlying pattern which explains, in part, some of the variability. The results therefore provide stronger evidence of the link between promotion and demand in international tourism than has been previously the case.

INTRODUCTION

Since 1950, total international tourist arrivals have grown by an average of about 7.4 percent per year. In terms of the number of arrivals,

Dr. Geoffrey I. Crouch is Associate Professor in the Faculty of Management and the World Tourism Education and Research Centre, The University of Calgary, 2500 University Drive, N.W., Calgary, Alberta T2N 1N4, Canada.

[Haworth co-indexing entry note]: "Promotion and Demand in International Toursim." Crouch, Geoffrey I. Co-published simultaneously in the *Journal of Travel & Tourism Marketing* (The Haworth Press, Inc.) Vol. 3, No. 3, 1994, pp. 109-125; and: *Economic Psychology of Travel and Tourism* (ed: John C. Crotts, and W. Fred van Raaij), The Haworth Press, Inc., 1994, pp. 109-125. Multiple copies of this article/chapter may be purchased from The Haworth Document Delivery Center [1-800-3-HAWORTH; 9:00 a.m. - 5:00 p.m. (EST)].

international travel is now about 16 times larger. It represents 7 percent of world export receipts and 20 percent of world service exports. All forecasts point to continued strong growth (World Tourism Organization, 1990).

As international tourism has grown, so has the interest in, and recognition of, this phenomenon as a significant area of economic activity. Today, nations compete aggressively for a share of the international travel and tourism market. This increased competition is evident in the expansion of the tourism infrastructure and superstructure; the development and staging of festivals and special events to attract tourists; the internationalization of tourism enterprises; the recognition of tourism at international forums which deal with international trade (such as the GATT); and the intensification of marketing programs in general, and promotion in particular, of countries as destinations.

International tourism involves *complex buying behaviour* (Kotler, 1988, p. 191). Consumers of international travel and tourism are *highly involved* in the purchase. International tourism is usually quite expensive and, for most people, is engaged in infrequently. Indeed, an international trip may be a once-in-a-lifetime experience, many years in the planning. It can be very risky and is certainly highly self-expressive. For many travelers, the anticipation of the trip, and the lingering memories and opportunities for "dinner party" stories, may be as significant as the trip itself. There are also *significant differences between destinations* (brands) requiring substantial information-gathering and evaluation behaviour tempered by beliefs and attitudes about countries which are often quite acute. In international marketing, perhaps the closest similarities are foreign educational services and health services.

As noted above, the promotion of countries as tourist destinations has intensified considerably. In more recent years, however, National Tourist Offices (NTOs) in particular have come under increased scrutiny to demonstrate the success of their promotional campaigns and thereby to justify industry and government funding. However, the link between promotion and demand is not easy to measure. Organizations which must compete for their survival know that promotion is important, but only vaguely understand how promotion works. There is a sense that, while some promotion can be highly effective, promotion involves much guess-work, "gut feel," and trial and error. Indeed, some promotion is probably quite ineffective, but it is very difficult to really know what does and doesn't work because so many influences can affect demand that, unless the promotion is subject to experimental control, it is almost impossible to apportion the variance in demand to its possible causes. This study seeks to examine the empirical evidence of the relationship between promotion and demand in the context of international tourism.

THE PROMOTION OF INTERNATIONAL TOURISM

International tourism is promoted in a wide variety of ways by a wide variety of organizations. Airlines, travel agents, tour operators, resorts, convention and visitor bureaus, hotels, and NTOs, for example, promote international travel and tourism individually and in collaborative arrangements. Therefore, "it is important to differentiate between country-of-origin marketing, which is largely private sector, tour operator led, and destination country marketing, which is often public sector, national tourism organization driven" (Witt, Brooke, and Buckley, 1991, p. 80).

Promotion might be targeted at either consumers or the travel trade. Consumer promotions have typically relied on brochures and print advertising in newspapers and magazines. For some time airlines have used television as the medium and more recently, the budgets of NTOs have enabled the mass television advertising of destinations. Publicity has been used to great effect as well. Many countries operate a program for visiting journalists. Such programs have been found to be particularly cost-effective, and can generate publicity which in value, exceeds the total annual budget of the sponsoring NTO.

Trade promotions have also become increasingly important. Travel trade shows; and corporate, incentive, and convention travel markets have grown in significance. Governments have opened travel offices in major origin markets, hence, the full promotional mix (viz. advertising, sales promotion, personal selling, and publicity) is now used extensively to promote international travel and tourism.

The focus in this study, however, is on destination promotion and the extent to which the programs of NTOs have boosted demand. The main marketing function of NTOs is the promotion of inbound international tourism, although promotion is only one element of the marketing mix. As international travel and tourism has grown, the promotional budgets of NTOs have risen significantly (World Tourism Organization, 1986; Lavery, 1992).

EVALUATING PROMOTIONAL EFFECTS

As promotional expenditure has increased, the need for, and interest in, methods which measure the impact of promotional expenditure on demand has generated much attention among practitioners and academic researchers (Australian Tourism Commission, 1991; Pizam, 1990; Toepper and Burke, 1991; Witt and Martin, 1987; Woodside, 1990.) A variety of approaches are possible including, for example, experimentation (Woodside, 1990), conversion studies (Burke and Gitelson, 1990), and tracking studies (Siegel and Ziff-Levine, 1990). Indeed, the evaluation of the Australian Tourism Commission's marketing impact used a "weight of evidence" approach by applying a variety of research and analytical methods rather than relying on the findings of any one study.

Some studies have applied regression analysis to relate changes in the demand for inbound international tourism to changes in promotional expenditure while at the same time accounting for the impact of other possible demand determinants. Although regression analysis is often referred to as causal modeling, the method, as normally applied, measures only the association between variables. Cause and effect might be inferred from any association but is not proven unless the data happens to have been derived using experimental control to distinguish cause from effect.

Few studies have estimated the impact of promotion on demand. The lack or unavailability of relevant data is the principal reason. Marketing expenditures by NTOs in response to competitive pressures and a wider recognition of the economic advantages of a strong tourism industry, have typically increased over time. The result is often a collinear relationship with incomes in origin markets (which have also typically increased over time) which confounds estimated demand elasticities. This, too, seems to have deterred some analysts from investigating the effect of marketing (Tremblay, 1989, p. 484).

Studies which have attempted to investigate the issue have ignored matters of promotional effectiveness, turning their attention to quantity rather than quality considerations. In most cases, the *amount* spent by NTOs on destination promotion was used as the measure for promotion. Promotions by national airlines and national tourism industries have been ignored. Again, lack of data has been the principal reason.

The results of these regression studies have been mixed (Sauran, 1978, p. 3). Some studies have found little or no measurable effect. For example, Uysal (1985, p. 58), in a study of destination marketing by Turkey, concluded that promotion was not an important factor. Barry and O'Hagan (1972) found no clear result for the impact of promotion by Bord Failte—the Irish tourist office. On the other hand, the work by Papadopoulos (1985, p. 690), in studying the effectiveness of promotional spending by the Greek national tourist office, obtained a significantly positive effect with an estimated advertising elasticity ranging between 0 and 1.6. Papadopoulos assessed the impact of total promotional expenditure, advertising expenditure, and public relations expenditure. Advertising appeared to have the greater explanatory power. A significant positive result was also produced by Clarke (1978, p. 93) in a study on travel to Barbados. Promotional expenditure was found to be highly significant in most cases, with a demand elasticity below one. He incorrectly concluded, however, that an inelastic result meant that the returns did not justify the expense. Such a conclusion would have required the conversion of the elasticity into a benefit/cost ratio on the basis of the current levels of promotion and tourist receipts. Sunday and Johansson (1975, p. 81) also found advertising to have a significant positive effect on travel to the USA. Contrary to the opinion of many researchers, they concluded that the effect of marketing did not carry over to the next year. They also found that the effectiveness of advertising varies between origin countries, appearing to decrease as a function of distance between the origin and destination.

Crouch, Schultz and Valerio (1992) also applied regression analysis to study the effect of promotion on inbound tourism to Australia from five origins; U.S.A., Japan, New Zealand, the United Kingdom and West Germany. They estimated demand elasticities varying in the range +0.11 and +0.25. The results were quite consistent in terms of sign and magnitude. They also converted these elasticities into benefit/cost ratios to estimate the increase in tourism receipts per dollar increase in promotion and found benefit/cost ratios varying between 9:1 (for the U.S.A.) and 220:1 (for New Zealand).

From among the five studies known to the author to have estimated promotional elasticities of demand for international tourism, a total of 197 elasticities have been derived (see Table 1). These estimates vary in terms of the country-of-origin, country-of-destination, time period, the definitions of the modeled variables, and other estimation characteristics. Although the number of studies is limited at this time, it is nevertheless useful to examine the differences among the estimates for underlying patterns in order to draw some generalizations, where possible.

HYPOTHESES

Promotional effort by a destination country and the demand for inbound international tourism to that country ought to be positively correlated (i.e., the promotional elasticity of demand ought to have a positive sign), after allowing for the effect of other causal factors. This is a reasonable assumption as one would expect higher demand to result from higher promotion. However, it is possible that the amount allocated to NTOs for promotions in origin markets might have been influenced by changes in demand over

TABLE 1. Available Estimates of Promotional Elasticities of Demand.

Study	Year	Number of Estimates	Comments
Barry & O'Hagan	1972	4	British travel to Ireland and promotion by Bord Failte.
Clarke	1978	63	USA, Canada, Trinidad and UK travel to Barbados and promotion broken down by season, class of hotel, and country of origin.
Crouch, Schultz and Valerio	1992	72	USA, Japan, New Zealand, UK and West German travel to Australia and promotion by the Australian Tourist Commission.
Papadopoulos	1985	36	Travel from Austria, West Germany, Sweden, the UK, Japan, France, Italy, Switzerland, and the USA to Greece, and promotion by Greece's National Tourist Office.
Uysal	1983	22	Travel from Greece, Yugoslavia, Italy, France, Spain, Austria, Switzerland, West Germany, the UK, Canada, and the USA to Turkey, and promotion by the Ministry of Tourism and Culture, Turkey.

time. For example, if demand had shown strong growth, governments may have been encouraged to increase expenditure on marketing to capitalise on this growth and reap greater economic rewards. A positive elasticity would still be the result but not for the usually argued reason. On the other hand, if a country increases marketing expenditure in order to respond to a decline in demand or increased competition among destinations, a negative elasticity could arise. Such a result, however, would more likely indicate a misspecified model which does not account for the real reasons for the decline in demand. The following hypothesis is therefore proposed.

H1: *The sign of the average estimated promotional elasticity of demand is positive.*

A number of inter-study characteristics might explain why estimated promotional elasticities vary from study to study. As noted above, it is possible that the way in which the model has been specified might bias the estimated elasticity. Paraskevopoulos (1977, p. 48) showed how estimates might be biased if relevant explanatory variables are omitted from the demand model forcing those explanatory variables which are present to account for the impact of the missing variable(s). Such a bias would occur if the omitted variable, and the variable for which the estimate is being made, are collinear.

H2: *The estimated promotional elasticity of demand varies as a function of the inclusion and omission of important explanatory variables.*

All models which were used to estimate promotional elasticities employed the log-linear (i.e., multiplicative) form. As studies were consistent in their approach on this aspect, the model form can not explain any of the variance in the estimates.

Characteristics of the study environment might also explain some of the variation among findings. Promotional elasticities may vary over time, for example. "It is quite likely that there have been some fundamental shifts in response of demand to other variables since the 1960s. These may have arisen from the major changes in fare structures, increased promotion and consequent high growth in travel. The economic upheavals of the mid and late 1970s also would have contributed to any shift in demand relationships. Elasticities are generally thought to remain stable only over limited periods and for relatively small changes in the economic environment" (Hollander, 1982, p. 44).

H3: *Estimates of promotional elasticities have varied over time.*

Estimated elasticities are also likely to vary by the tourist's country-of-origin. Different cultures may respond differently to a destination country's promotions. Prevailing attitudes and perceptions; cultural, religious and immigration ties; and knowledge of the destination country are antecedents to the way in which markets respond to promotion. Tremblay (1989, p. 487) in a cross-sectional study, used dummy variables to allow demand elasticities to vary by country of origin. He found the country dummy variables to be highly statistically significant.

H4: *The estimated effect of promotion on demand depends upon the country-of-origin of the tourists involved.*

Similarly, the nature of the destination might also affect estimates. Demand is likely to be more responsive to promotion where the conditions are favourable to inbound tourism but the tourist markets lack sufficient information about the destination. On the other hand, no amount of promotion is likely to stimulate significantly travel to a destination which suffers from civil strife, terrorism, or some other major deterrent. Changing travel tastes or fashions (the so-called destination life cycle) may also influence the impact of promotion on demand.

H5: *The estimated promotional elasticity of demand varies as a function of the destination country involved.*

Hypotheses 4 and 5 also suggest the possibility that the effect of promotion might differ depending on the length of haul involved. As the "information gap" is likely to be greater in the case of long-haul travel there may be greater scope for promotion to influence demand in such cases. Tourists typically know much more about their neighbouring countries as destinations, but may possess quite biased or inaccurate impressions of destinations which are much further from home. Under these conditions, promotions can be more informative and have the potential to significantly improve the level of awareness of long-haul destinations.

H6: *International tourism demand is more sensitive to the promotion of destinations in which long-haul travel is required.*

Studies also differed in terms of the characteristics of the data analyzed. Demand was measured in three alternative ways; (1) expenditure/receipts, (2) arrivals/departures, or (3) the number of tourist nights. The effect of promotion on demand may therefore depend on the measure of demand used in the study. Tourists might respond to promotion in a variety of ways, either by visiting the particular destination rather than some other alternative destination, by increasing expenditure per day, or by staying longer.

H7: *The effect of promotion on demand depends upon the way in which demand is defined.*

Finally, the method used to solve model equations for the estimated elasticities can yield different results. Some studies used ordinary least-squares regression while others employed the Cochrane-Orcutt procedure to correct for serial correlation. Assmus, Farley and Lehmann (1984, p. 68) discuss estimation-method bias and note that "there is ambiguity about how estimation method might affect estimated parameters."

H8: *Estimated promotional elasticities of demand vary as a function of the estimation method used.*

METHODOLOGY

The traditional narrative review of literature is open to considerable criticism (Hunter, Schmidt and Jackson 1982, p. 129). Over the last fifteen years or so, meta-analytical methods have been developed to address many of the short-comings of the traditional narrative technique (e.g., see Hunter et al., 1982). The method uses a statistical perspective to identify underlying patterns in the findings, and to correct the distribution of findings for study artifacts, the most important being variance due to sampling error. That is, some or all of the variation in findings (i.e., in this study the estimated promotional elasticities) may occur as a result of sampling error and other artifactual effects. If the results are corrected to account for the artifactual effects one would find more agreement among the results.

A procedure for correcting results obtained from regression studies has been developed by Raju, Fralicx and Steinhaus (1986). This method was used to investigate the variation in results across the set of empirical studies. Three steps were involved in the analysis as follows:

1. an examination of the frequency distribution of estimated promotional elasticities, including a t-test on the mean of the distributions,
2. the mean and variance of the elasticities, corrected for study artifacts was then calculated using the Raju procedure to establish whether the variation in results across studies was real or whether it was apparently due to artifactual effects,

3. where inter-study factors appear to be important, the Raju procedure was then used to estimate the corrected mean and variance of elasticities for each subset as defined by the hypotheses discussed above.

Raju et al. show that the mean (M_B) and variance (V_B) of B (the estimated elasticity or regression slope) can be estimated as follows:

$$M_B = \frac{M_b}{M_{rel}}$$

and

$$V_B = \frac{V_b - V_e - \left(\dfrac{M_b}{M_{rel}}\right)^2 V_{rel}}{V_{rel} + M_{rel}^2}$$

where: M_b = mean of the observed regression coefficients obtained from several validity studies,

V_b = variance of the same observed regression coefficients,
M_{rel} = mean of the predictor reliability
V_{rel} = variance of the predictor reliability, and
V_e = sampling variance.

RESULTS AND DISCUSSION

The frequency distribution of the estimated promotional elasticities is illustrated in Figure 1. The mean of the distribution is +0.31 with a standard deviation of 0.30. The mean is statistically significantly different from zero at the 1 percent level (t-statistic = 14.61; t-probability = 0.000). The results are therefore consistent with Hypothesis 1.

The corrected mean, variance and standard deviation are +0.41, 0.09 and 0.30 respectively. Approximately 31 percent of the observed variance in the elasticities occurs as a result of sampling error. The substantial variance remaining after correction for sampling error and other study artifacts points to the effect of moderator variables.

The results of the meta-analysis are reported in Table 2. The columns headed *Variable Class, Variable,* and *Level* relate to the various hypotheses developed earlier. The column headed *Mean Elasticity* represents the mean of the estimated promotional elasticities for each hypothesis subset, after correction for study artifacts using the Raju procedure. For example,

FIGURE 1. Frequency Distribution of Estimated Promotional Elasticities.

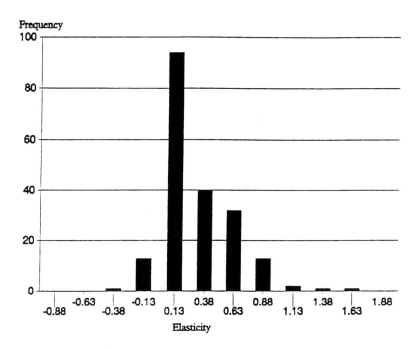

models which included income as an explanatory variable had an average corrected mean promotional elasticity of +0.40, compared to +0.60 for models which omitted income as a variable. That is, the omission of income appears to have positively biased the estimate of promotional elasticity. Over time, real incomes have typically increased. Expenditure on destination promotion has also generally risen. Incomes and promotion are therefore positively correlated. Therefore, if income is omitted from the model, the promotional variable is forced to carry some of the effect of income and this hypothesis is supported by the results.

In order to examine whether the mean elasticities of the subsets are statistically significantly different, F-statistics were calculated and compared to the value of F at the five percent level. For tests which involved more than two levels, the Scheffe test was used to identify which of the levels are statistically significantly different (last column of Table 2). The Scheffe test results are to be interpreted such that levels associated with the same alphabetic character are significantly different at the five percent level. In

TABLE 2. Meta-Analysis of Promotional Elasticities.

Variable Class	Variable	Level	Mean Elasticity M_B	F-statistic	$F_{0.05}$	Scheffe Test[a]
Model Specification	income	included	0.40	27.6	3.89	
		omitted	0.60			
	price	included	0.43	11.1	3.89	
		omitted	0.31			
	exchange rate	included	0.17	75.8	3.89	
		omitted	0.45			
	transportation cost	included	0.51	64.4	3.89	
		omitted	0.23			
Environmental Characteristics	time period (centricity)	1960-1965	0.20	332	2.26	a
		1965-1970	0.67			abcd
		1970-1975	0.07			b
		1975-1980	0.30			ce
		1980-1985	0.17			de
	nationality of tourists by country	Austria	0.03	18.4	1.80	abcd
		Sweden	0.17			ef
		Switzerland	0.04			ghi
		UK	0.30			jk
		France	0.82			aegilmno

Data Characteristics	destination country	USA	0.50			bpqv
		West Germany	0.32			ls
		Canada	0.75			cfhkpstuv
		Italy	0.13			mqtw
		Spain	0.54			
		Japan	0.28			nu
		New Zealand	0.20			orvx
		Other	0.54			diwx
		France	0.20	46.8	2.41	a
		Greece	0.39			bcd
		Australia	0.23			be
		Turkey	0.16			cf
		Barbados	0.67			adef
	length of haul	longer	0.25	97.0	3.04	
		shorter	0.17			
	demand measure	expenditure/receipts	0.11	138	3.04	ab
		arrivals/departures	0.27			ac
		tourist nights	0.67			bc
Estimation Method	technique	Ordinary least-squares	0.43	23.8	3.89	ab
		Cochrane-Orcutt	0.21			bc

*The mean elasticity is statistically significantly different at the 5 percent level where variable levels share the same alphabetic character.

the income-related example, the difference is significant as the F-statistic is greater than $F_{0.05}$.

In each case the omission of a price variable (i.e., the relative cost of travel and tourism services in the destination), an exchange rate variable, and a cost-of-transportation variable appear also to have biased the results. A bias indicates some correlation between the promotional variable and each of the omitted variables, but the reason for such a relationship is not evident. It may simply be a function of data employed in each study.

Average promotional elasticities also vary by time period, nationality of the tourists, country of destination, and length of haul. However, there appears to be no discernable pattern based on the time period of the study. Tourists from France and Spain appear to be the most sensitive to destination promotions, whereas, the Austrians and Swiss appear to be least affected. As destinations, Barbados and Greece display the highest elasticities, while France and Turkey are associated with lower values. Again, there is no obvious explanation for this pattern.

As hypothesized, long-haul travel appears to be more sensitive to promotional expenditure. Promotion also seems to influence the number of tourist nights to a greater extent than arrivals/departures or expenditures/receipts implying that promotion convinces tourists to stay longer but not necessarily to spend much more.

Finally, the average estimated promotional elasticity of demand is higher when the ordinary least-squares method was used. As noted above, however, the nature of estimation-method bias is not clear.

The possible interpretations of the results of Table 2 are highly speculative. Although the set of estimated promotional elasticities is quite large, they were derived from only five separate studies. More empirical studies are therefore needed to increase the number of results by each combination of substantive and methodological inter-study characteristics. At present, however, it is likely that some confounding of effects has occurred. Nevertheless, the results do indicate a significant positive association between promotion and demand, and provide some insight into the variation of estimates across studies.

CONCLUSION

National Tourist Offices and destination marketing organizations generally have never been more aware of the need to understand and measure the effect of their promotional activity on demand. Much more research is required, however, before this complex relationship can be more deeply understood. Governments and the tourism industry will, it is certain, become increasingly demanding in seeking justification for funding of destination promotions.

This paper has identified a number of studies which have attempted to empirically estimate promotional elasticities of demand. The paper reviewed the findings and, through the use of meta-analysis, provides some indication of how and why findings vary from study to study. There is some evidence to suggest that the results depend upon the way in which the model is specified, the particular circumstances being modeled, the way in which the variables are defined, and the estimation method employed. It is obvious, therefore, that care should be exercised when using empirical estimates of the effect of tourism promotion on demand; that is, estimates should not be used out of context. Nevertheless, the hypotheses supported in this study provide some basis for generalizing the results as follows:

1. *There is a positive association between promotion and demand.* The mean promotional elasticity of demand (corrected for sampling error) is +0.41. On this basis an increase in demand of 0.41% would be associated with an increase in the promotional budget of the NTO of 1%.
2. *Ignoring the impact of other important demand determinants may produce spurious results.* Elasticity estimates are biased when collinear determinants are omitted from the demand model.
3. *The sensitivity of demand to promotion varies spatially.* The residents of some nations display a higher sensitivity to tourism promotion than those from other nations. This promotional sensitivity may depend also on the destination being promoted, and its relationship with the origin country. For example, the length of haul between the two countries, the nature and extent of existing cultural and trade ties, and levels of awareness or ignorance may all be important factors.
4. *Promotion may influence length of stay more than it influences total expenditure.* An increased desire to visit a country can be expressed either by attracting more visitors, by persuading visitors to consume more expensive, higher value, tourism services, or by convincing them to stay longer.

Until some real scientific experimentation, as called for by Woodside (1990), is carried out, however, the causal relationship between promotion and demand will remain speculative. In particular, the question of whether promotional budgets are set independently of changes in demand requires further investigation if associative rather than experimental methods are to be relied upon.

Although promotional elasticities of demand provide useful information, they do not answer directly the question of whether benefits exceed costs. Future empirical studies should therefore estimate benefit/cost ratios by relating elasticities to the amount spent on promotion and the receipts from tourist expenditure. Information in this form would indicate whether promotions produce adequate rewards, and how total promotional budgets might be allocated among different origin markets.

Another important question concerns the allocation of promotional spending among different elements of the promotional mix (i.e., advertising, publicity, sales promotion, and personal selling), and among different messages and modes. Other than through conversion and tracking studies, which usually stop short of assessing the effects on actual visitation, little is known about the qualitative side of national tourism promotion. Similarly, almost nothing is known about the effect of country-of-origin, private-sector/tour-operator led marketing on international tourism demand. Nor has the symbiosis between private-sector and public-sector destination promotion ever been studied in any detail. There is considerable scope for further research in this area.

REFERENCES

Assmus, Gert, John U. Farley and Donald Lehmann (1984). How advertising affects sales: A meta-analysis of econometric results. *Journal of Marketing Research*, 21 (1): 65-74.

Australian Tourist Commission (1991). *Evaluation of the Australian Tourist Commission's marketing impact*. Sydney, Australia: Author.

Barry, Kevin and John O'Hagan (1972). An econometric study of British tourist expenditure in Ireland. *Economic and Social Review*, 3 (2): 143-161.

Burke, James F. and Richard Gitelson (1990). Conversion studies: Assumptions, applications, accuracy and abuse. *Journal of Travel Research*, 28 (3): 46-50.

Clarke, Carl D. (1978). *An analysis of the determinants of demand for tourism in Barbados*, Ph.D. dissertation, Fordham University.

Crouch, Geoffrey I., Lance Schultz and Peter Valerio (1992). Marketing international tourism to Australia–A regression analysis. *Tourism Management*, 13 (2): 196-208.

Hollander, G. (1982). *Determinants of Demand for Travel to and from Australia*. Australia: Bureau of Industry Economics, Working Paper No. 26.

Hunter, John E., Frank L. Schmidt and Gregg B. Jackson (1982). *Meta-Analysis: Cumulating Research Findings Across Studies*, Beverly Hills, California: Sage Publications Inc.

Kotler, Philip (1988). *Marketing Management: Analysis, Planning, Implementation, and Control*. Sixth edition, Englewood Cliffs, NJ: Prentice-Hall.

Lavery, Patrick (1992). The financing and organization of National Tourist Offices, *Travel & Tourism Analyst*, No. 4: 84-101.

Papadopoulos, Socrates I. (1985). *An economic analysis of foreign tourism to Greece, 1960-1984, with a planning model and marketing policy recommendations*, Ph.D. dissertation, University of Bradford, UK.

Paraskevopoulos, George N. (1977). *An Econometric Analysis of International Tourism.* Athens, Greece: Center of Planning and Economic Research.

Pizam, Abraham (1990). Evaluating the effectiveness of travel trade shows and other tourism sales-promotion techniques. *Journal of Travel Research*, 29 (1): 3-8.

Raju, Nambury S., Rodney Fralicx and Stephen D. Steinhaus (1986). Covariance and regression slope models for studying validity generalization. *Applied Psychological Measurement*, 10 (2): 195-211.

Sauran, Alan (1978). Economic determinants of tourist demand: A survey. *The Tourist Review*, 3 (1): 2-4.

Siegel, William and William Ziff-Levine (1990). Evaluating tourism advertising campaigns: Conversion vs. advertising tracking studies. *Journal of Travel Research*, 28 (3): 51-55.

Sunday, Alexander A. and Johny K. Johansson (1975). Advertising and international tourism: In *Management Science Applications to Leisure-Time Operations*, (pp. 81-96). Shaul Ladany, (Ed.), Amsterdam: North-Holland Publishing Co.

Toepper, Lorin K. and James F. Burke (1991). *Accountability Research: Getting the Right Numbers and Getting the Numbers Right*. Washington, D.C.: U.S. Department of Commerce Task Force on Accountability Research and the Travel and Tourism Research Association.

Tremblay, Pascal (1989). Pooling international tourism in western Europe. *Annals of Tourism Research*, 16 (4): 477-491.

Uysal, Muzaffer (1983). Construction of a model which investigates the impact of selected variables on international tourist flows to Turkey, Ph.D. dissertation, Texas A&M University.

Witt, Stephen F. and Christine A. Martin (1987). International tourism demand models–Inclusion of marketing variables. *Tourism Management*, 8 (1): 33-40.

Witt, Stephen F., Michael Z. Brooke and Peter J. Buckley (1991). *The Management of International Tourism*. London: Unwin Hyman.

Woodside, Arch G. (1990). Measuring advertising effectiveness in destination marketing strategies. *Journal of Travel Research*, 29 (2): 3-8.

World Tourism Organization (1986). *Budgets of National Tourism Administrations*. Madrid, Spain: Author.

World Tourism Organization (1990). *Tourism to the Year 2000: Qualitative Aspects Affecting Global Growth*. Madrid, Spain: Author.

Index

Adaptation during decision making
  process, 72-73
Advertising
  affective, cognitive factors
    interaction in, 11
  behaviorism and, 5
  effects of, 11
  See also Direct mail; International
    tourism, promotion, demand
    research in; Tour brochures
    experiential information
    research
Affect (emotion) on consumer
  behavior, 6
AIHP. *See* America's Industrial
  Heritage Project (AIHP)
Allocentric novelty-seeking
  typology, 49
America's Industrial Heritage Project
  (AIHP), 62
Attitudes influencing consumer
  behavior, ix
Australia international tourism
  research results, 113,114,121
Australian Tourism Commission,
  112,114

Barbados international tourism
  research results, 114,121,
  122
Behavior. *See* Behaviorism;
  Consumer behavior
Behaviorism
  advertising and, 5
  decision process models and,
    72-73
  optimal arousal theory and, 5-6
  product reinforcement and, 5

social learning and, 5
See also Economic psychology
Bounded rationality, 4
Business tax compliance behavior,
  11

Chain identity, in tourism
  organizations, 33
Changing lifestyles influencing
  decision making, 50
Children influencing decision
  making, 50
  See also Family
Club Med, 32
Cognitive psychology
  economic psychology
    interdiscipline with, 1
  learning, choice, memory
    processes and, 6
  Lewin's field theory in, 6
  mental imagery process types
    and, 93-94,101-102
Commitment
  ego involvement and, 45
  loyalty and, 43-44
    Psychological Commitment
    Instrument (PCI) and, 44
Conjoint choice decision making
  model, 70,71
Constructive processing, 94
Consumer behavior, 10
  affect (emotion) and, 6
  attitudes, motivation, social
    influences on, ix, 10
  goals, values of, 22-24
  motivation and, 4
  decision making process models
    and, 72-73

127

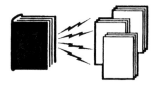 **Haworth**

DOCUMENT DELIVERY
SERVICE

This new service provides a single-article order form for any article from a Haworth journal.

- *Time Saving:* No running around from library to library to find a specific article.
- *Cost Effective:* All costs are kept down to a minimum.
- *Fast Delivery:* Choose from several options, including same-day FAX.
- *No Copyright Hassles:* You will be supplied by the original publisher.
- *Easy Payment:* Choose from several easy payment methods.

Open Accounts Welcome for ...
- Library Interlibrary Loan Departments
- Library Network/Consortia Wishing to Provide Single-Article Services
- Indexing/Abstracting Services with Single Article Provision Services
- Document Provision Brokers and Freelance Information Service Providers

---

MAIL or FAX THIS ENTIRE ORDER FORM TO:

Attn: **Marianne Arnold**
Haworth Document Delivery Service
The Haworth Press, Inc.
10 Alice Street
Binghamton, NY 13904-1580

or **FAX:** (607) 722-1424
or **CALL:** 1-800-3-HAWORTH
(1-800-342-9678; 9am-5pm EST)

PLEASE SEND ME PHOTOCOPIES OF THE FOLLOWING SINGLE ARTICLES:

1) Journal Title: _____

    Vol/Issue/Year: _____ Starting & Ending Pages: _____

Article Title: _____

_____

2) Journal Title: _____

    Vol/Issue/Year: _____ Starting & Ending Pages: _____

Article Title: _____

_____

3) Journal Title: _____

    Vol/Issue/Year: _____ Starting & Ending Pages: _____

Article Title: _____

_____

4) Journal Title: _____

    Vol/Issue/Year: _____ Starting & Ending Pages: _____

Article Title: _____

(See other side for Costs and Payment Information)

COSTS: Please figure your cost to order quality copies of an article.

1. Set-up charge per article: $8.00
   ($8.00 × number of separate articles) _____

2. Photocopying charge for each article:
   1-10 pages: $1.00 _____

   11-19 pages: $3.00 _____

   20-29 pages: $5.00 _____

   30+ pages: $2.00/10 pages _____

3. Flexicover (optional): $2.00/article _____

4. Postage & Handling: US: $1.00 for the first article/
   $.50 each additional article _____

   Federal Express: $25.00 _____

   Outside US: $2.00 for first article/
   $.50 each additional article _____

5. Same-day FAX service: $.35 per page _____

GRAND TOTAL: _____

METHOD OF PAYMENT: (please check one)

❑ Check enclosed ❑ Please ship and bill. PO # _____
(sorry we can ship and bill to bookstores only! All others must pre-pay)

❑ Charge to my credit card: ❑ Visa; ❑ MasterCard; ❑ American Express;

Account Number: _____ Expiration date: _____

Signature: ✗_____ Name: _____

Institution: _____ Address: _____

City: _____ State: _____ Zip: _____

Phone Number: _____ FAX Number: _____

MAIL or *FAX* THIS ENTIRE ORDER FORM TO:

Attn: **Marianne Arnold**
Haworth Document Delivery Service
The Haworth Press, Inc.
10 Alice Street
Binghamton, NY 13904-1580

or FAX: (607) 722-1424
or CALL: 1-800-3-HAWORTH
(1-800-342-9678; 9am-5pm EST)